Voice of Senses

Other books of interest

1. **भारतीय परम्परा में मृत्यु की अवधारणा** – शरीर का अन्तरण और दाहकर्म संस्कार — लेखक ज्यान ज्युसेप्पे फिलिप्पी, अनुवादक बी॰एल॰ धीमान, सम्पादक ज्यान्नी पेल्लेगीनी, ISBN 81-246-0313-8.
2. **Mṛtyu, Concept of Death in Indian Traditions** — Transformation of the Body and Funeral Rites; by G.G. Filippi; ISBN 81-246-0072-4.
3. **मृत्यु की दस्तक** – प्राचीन शास्त्र एवं आधुनिक ज्ञान, सम्पादक बैद्यनाथ सरस्वती, रामलखन मौर्य, ISBN 81-246-0314-6.
4. **Voice of Death** — Traditional Thought and Modern Science; edited by Baidyanath Saraswati; ISBN 81-246-0274-3.
5. **Voice of Life** — Traditional Thought and Modern Science; edited by Baidyanath Saraswati; ISBN 81-246-0366-9.

Voice of Senses

Traditional Thought and Modern Science

Edited by
Baidyanath Saraswati

D.K. Printworld (P) Ltd.
New Delhi

in association with

N.K. Bose Memorial Foundation
Varanasi

Cataloging in Publication Data — DK
[Courtesy: D.K. Agencies (P) Ltd. <docinfo@dkagencies.com>]

Voice of senses : traditional thought and modern science / edited by Baidyanath Saraswati.
ix, 238 p. 23 cm.
Contributed articles.
Includes bibliographical references.
Includes index.
ISBN 8124604096

1. Sense (Philosophy). 2. Senses and sensation — Religious aspects. 3. Senses and sensation — Social aspects. 4. Science and civilization. I. Saraswati, Baidyanath, 1932-, II. N.K. Bose Memorial Foundation.

DDC 121.35 22

ISBN 81-246-0409-6
First Published in India in 2007

Published by:
D.K. Printworld (P) Ltd.
Regd. office : *'Sri Kunj'*, F-52, Bali Nagar, New Delhi - 110 015
Phones : (011) 2545-3975; 2546-6019; *Fax* : (011) 2546-5926
E-mail : dkprintworld@vsnl.net *Web* : www.dkprintworld.com

in association with

N.K. Bose Memorial Foundation
B-8/9, Bara Gambhir Singh, Varanasi - 221001 (UP)
Phone : (0542) 2275289; *E-mail* : nkbfoundation@yahoo.com

Printed by: D.K. Printworld (P) Ltd., New Delhi.

Contents

Key to Transliteration

VOWELS

अ *a*	आ *ā*	इ *i*	ई *ī*	उ *u*	ऊ *ū*
(b<u>u</u>t)	(p<u>a</u>lm)	(<u>i</u>t)	(b<u>ee</u>t)	(p<u>u</u>t)	(p<u>oo</u>l)
ऋ *ṛ*	ए *e*	ऐ *ai*	ओ *o*	औ *au*	
(<u>rhy</u>thm)	(pla<u>y</u>)	(<u>ai</u>r)	(t<u>oe</u>)	(l<u>ou</u>d)	

CONSONANTS

Guttural	क *ka*	ख* *kha*	ग *ga*	घ *gha*	ङ *ṅa*
	(s<u>k</u>ate)	(bloc<u>kh</u>ead)	(<u>g</u>ate)	(<u>gh</u>ost)	(si<u>ng</u>)
Palatal	च *ca*	छ* *cha*	ज *ja*	झ *jha*	ञ *ña*
	(<u>ch</u>unk)	(cat<u>ch h</u>im)	(<u>j</u>ohn)	(hed<u>geh</u>og)	(bu<u>n</u>ch)
Cerebral	ट *ṭa*	ठ* *ṭha*	ड *ḍa*	ढ* *ḍha*	ण* *ṇa*
	(s<u>t</u>art)	(an<u>th</u>ill)	(<u>d</u>art)	(go<u>dh</u>ead)	(u<u>n</u>der)
Dental	त *ta*	थ *tha*	द *da*	ध* *dha*	न *na*
	(pa<u>th</u>)	(<u>th</u>under)	(<u>th</u>at)	(brea<u>the</u>)	(<u>n</u>umb)
Labial	प *pa*	फ* *pha*	ब *ba*	भ *bha*	म *ma*
	(s<u>p</u>in)	(<u>ph</u>iloso<u>ph</u>y)	(<u>b</u>in)	(a<u>bh</u>or)	(<u>m</u>uch)
Semi-	य *ya*	र *ra*	ल *la*	व *va*	
vowels	(<u>y</u>oung)	(d<u>r</u>ama)	(<u>l</u>uck)	(<u>v</u>ile)	
Sibilants	श *śa*	ष *ṣa*	स *sa*	ह *ha*	
	(<u>sh</u>ove)	(bu<u>sh</u>el)	(<u>s</u>o)	(<u>h</u>um)	
Others	क्ष *kṣa*	त्र *tra*	ज्ञ *jña*	ळ* ḷ	ॠ* *ṝ*
	(*<u>kṣa</u>triya*)	(*<u>tri</u>śūla*)	(*<u>jñā</u>nī*)	(*p<u>la</u>y*)	

अं (ं) *ṁ anusvāra* (nasalisation of preceding vowel) like *sa<u>ṁ</u>skṛti*

अः *visarga* = *ḥ* (aspiration of preceding vowel) like (*prāta<u>ḥ</u>*)

ऽ *Avagraha* consonant #'consonant (like:- *ime 'vasthitā*)

Anusvāra at the end of a line is presented by m (म्) and not ṁ

HINDI LETTERS (extras)

ँ = *ñ* (*candrabindu*) ं = ṅ (*anusvāra*) ड़ = *ṛa* ढ़ = *ṛha*

* No exact English equivalents for these letters.

Introduction

Baidyanath Saraswati

THE N.K. Bose Memorial Seminar on *Traditional Thought and Modern Science* began with the Concept of Death (November 2002), followed by the Concept of Life (November 2003). Both pervade all human thinking : death symbolizes zero, life flickers. The third in this series, was devoted to the Concept of Senses (November 2004), also a universal theme, building up the chemistry of life. The recurring cycle of Five senses is a frequent one, especially in classical Chinese, Tibetan thought and Indian philosophy.

Theme

The theory of Five Elements or Five Processes is basic to Chinese tradition. The Elements referred to are the Wood, Fire, Earth, Metal and Water. They are not so much the material substances that we would commonly associate with those Five names, as a reference to Five kinds of processes, which explain the composition of the physical world. It is really a description of how the material world forms and changes. In Chinese culture, there are Five tastes: sour, bitter, sweet, metallic and salty; Five emotions: anger, joy, anxiety, grief and fear; Five colours: blue, red, yellow, white and black; Five directions: north, south, east, west, and with obvious logic centre; and Five kinds of climate: windy, hot, dry, humid and cold. It would be more appropriate to describe the Five elements as the Five Processes. The Chinese theory of *yin* and *yang* forms a harmonious whole. Everything in the universe is either *yin* or *yang* — the world itself, the objects in the world, the mankind, the parts of the body, the functions of those parts and the medical condition which affect those functions. Neither *yin* nor *yang* is absolute. Even the most *yin* thing has a small element of *yang* within it and vice versa. That is why the symbol of the relationship of *yin* and *yang* looks as it does. It reminds us that because *yin* and *yang* are always changing, *yin* can become *yang* and *yang* can become *yin*, according to the flux of the universe. Nothing in this world is fixed and immutable.

The Five aggregates comprehended in Tibetan thoughts, are taken as being naturally and wholly voidness. Forms are voidness and voidness is Form, nor are Forms and voidness separable, or Forms other than voidness. In the same way, perception, feeling, volition and consciousness are voidness. Thus are all things voidness: without characteristics, unborn, unimpeded, unsullied, unsulliable, unsubtracted and unfilled. Such being so, voidness has no form, no perception, no feeling, no volition, no consciousness, no eyes, no ears, no nose, no tongue, no body, no mind, no form, no sound, no smell, no taste, no touch, no quality. Where there is no eye there is no desire, there is no consciousness of desire. There is no ignorance, there is no overcoming of ignorance, there is no decay and no death, and there is no overcoming of decay and death. In the same way, there is no sorrow, there is no evil, there is no taking away, there is no path, there is no wisdom, nor any attaining, nor not attaining. The Awakened One also realized concomitantly with his awakening, that all the other dualities, such as joy and sorrow, good and evil, adding to and taking away, are merely *sāṁsārika* hallucinations. So, too, for such a One there is no path, nor any traverser of the path. There is no wisdom, just as there is no ignorance, nor any attaining or not–attaining of wisdom. In short, there is nothing that the unlimited mind may conceive that which has other than an illusory, dualistic existence.

The recurring cycle of Five is a frequent one in Indian thought: the Five Buddha, the Five-headed Śiva, the Five-coloured thread, the Five consecration, the Five lamps, the Five leaves, the Five nectars, the Five offerings, the Five precepts, and the Five products of a cow have their own explication. The Five elements referring to Earth, Water, Fire, Air and Sky are not merely insentient elements but are a combination of both consciousness as also non-conscious principles. Elements are defined in the Vedic Sūkta. They have been regarded as divinities. To the Buddhists, the universal elements of matter are more energies than substances. The *Abhidharmakośa* explains this: The *rūpaskandha* consists of Five sense-organs (*indriyas*), their Five objects (*artha*) and unmanifested Act (*avijñapti*), and thus it is Elevenfold. The Five sense-organs are the eye, the ear, the nose, the tongue and the tactile organ. The Five objects are the objects of these very sense-organs, namely the visible, the sound, the taste, the odour and the tangible. It is further said that the subtle material Elements (*rūpaprasāda*), conveying visual and other sensations, which are the points of support for the respective consciousness of the visual, etc. are the Five sense-organs that organize human behaviour, develop aesthetic sense, and communicate knowledge of all kinds. The modes and matter of communication may vary from person to person, from culture to culture. Indian thought reflects a deeper concern towards "hearing" as the most exact way of communication. In fact, the entire knowledge system of the classical scholars, ranging from theology, philosophy, music and medicine (based on pulse reading), owes predominantly to the faculty of hearing.

In contrast to this, the Western thought is extremely *vision-oriented*. John Locke's famous dictum "the perception of the mind is most aptly explained by words relating to the sight" has proven one of the basic tenets of the empiricists in the Western world. Thus, what comes out is that: whereas the

East is extremely *hearing-oriented,* the West is extremely *vision-oriented.* This differential orientation of the people belonging to different cultures and civilizations invites our attention on understanding of how differently the Five sense-organs have been treated in various discipline and cultures.

This raises questions: Who sets the Five senses in order? Who is aware when a man is lost in sleep? How do we look at the individual Self? Is consciousness a universal manifesting field? Is it the primal condition of human nature and culture? Who provides hearing and seeing? Does hearing precede seeing? What is the difference between the hearing and the seeing? Is the hearing-oriented culture superior to the seeing-oriented culture? Where is the seed of the archaic? What has modern science to say about human senses? What do neuroscientists say about the faculties of telepathy and clairvoyance? How do people acquire the ability to sense magnetic fields associated with psychic presentiments such as prophetic and intuitional message and remote viewing? How does an artist view the Five senses? What has Āyurveda to say about the senses? What have other researchers to say about the human feelings and emotions? Do animals have the Five senses, as in humans? Do trees have human-like vibratory patterns?

Quite apart, there are non-literate people who read the nature of Nature, beyond the range of modern science. Here is an example: Before the recent massive tsunami, giant waves, that slammed into Sri Lanka and India, as reported in *National Geographic News* (January 4, 2005), the wild and domestic animals seemed to know what was about to happen, and so they fled to safety. According to eye-witness accounts, the following events happened: Elephants screamed and ran for higher grounds. Dogs refused to go outdoors. Flamingoes abandoned their low-lying breeding areas. Zoo animals rushed into their shelters, and could not be enticed to come out. The traditional belief that wild and domestic animals possess a *sixth sense,* and know in advance when the Earth is going to shake, has been around for centuries. A Jarwa (tribal) of the middle Andaman explained that there is a stark contrast between the amplitude and frequency of normal tidal waves and those of tsunami. The moment the first wave was spotted, the tribals knew what force was coming, and fled to the highlands. What is that knowledge which these *primitives* (uncivilized?) followed? It is called the *sixth sense.* However the gnosis of the modern masters failed. UN tsunami recovery envoy listened to the concern of victims — more than 217,000 dead around the Indian Ocean on December 26, 2004.

Is our understanding of the senses set in a low key? Will the Earth give way to a ghost melee? What is going on in the celestial world? Is man capable of providing a key to the origins of Life and Death? Can modern science and technology create Senses without Nature (Spirit)?

Voices

The voices create a climate of opinion. Reason and logic cry out in pain, but mankind has learnt not to bother too much with reason and logic. The faith determines the course of life, but at a certain moment it ceases to have determinable positions and often finds a way of moving up in two orbits. Or cling to what appears to be the substantial world, as defined in philosophy, religion, science and social life.

Philosophy and Religion

The dictionary definition of philosophy reads: "The rational investigation of being, knowledge and right conduct." The Sanskrit word for philosophy is *darśana* (sight), that is, "great thinking" or talking about what is "seen" and what is "unseen(?)." Grammatically, the English word "religion" comes from *re-legrere,* i.e. "gather," "collect." Philosophically it tends towards *re-ligare,* i.e. what unites, links up man to his divinity. The Sanskrit word *dharma* (Pāli, *dhamma*) is far more comprehensive than "religion." Derived from *dhṛ* (to hold, keep, maintain), it reflects in different contexts, such as attributes of mind, functions of the sense-organs, duty, nature of attributes, etc.

The Voice of Senses, raised in philosophy and religion, create a climate of faith. Scriptures sanctify faith. Oral tradition points out that the Universe consists of both matter and spirit. The body is made up of Five Elements or Senses. The Five Processes theory is basic to traditional thought in many parts of the world. An inquiry into the Senses is such that *Self-experience* does not drift away from traditional search for a universal principle. The philosophical thought creates "religious world-view," and holds "perceptual experiences," determining relationship between the two.

Sitansu Ray, a man tinted with the colour of Santiniketan, points out that Rabindranath Tagore's congregational addresses on *dekha* "seeing", and *shona* "hearing," lead us to the view that there are two reciprocal and complementary rules concerning the Five senses. Tagore, the great artist and humanist, starts with the phenomena of light, the main contingent for visual perception. Light provides the necessary condition of "seeing" the wonderful world of beautiful forms, the *rūper jharanā,* arising from the infinite ocean of beauty (*ananta rūpasāgara*). The poet Tagore feels that the grand cosmic orchestration along with decoration and dancing of everything in the Universe, is surcharged with the passion of love (*preme preme baje*), as it were.

Uma Marina Vesci, a distinguished Indologist, takes up the ancient Indian vision of the Senses. The Vedas and the Upaniṣads deal with the Senses as a powerful means of growing up in the world. Here the overall details of the Senses have been appreciably expanded in terms of subject-oriented studies, a remarkable shift in philosophical development.

Nirad Baran Mandal is convinced that from ancient times the sages grasped the Five senses, and gave a logical foundation to consciousness and seeing, without matter. He takes up the question of Mind: Is it *jñānendriya* or *karmendriya*? Also, there is a controversy about whether it is an *indriya*. Some refuse to accept Mind as an *indriya*. According to *Gītā*, Mind is the sixth sense. Following *Sāṁkhya Kārikā*, Mind is both *jñānendriya* and *karmendriya*. Buddhists and Jains also accept the Five senses.

S.K. Pathak deals with the key features of human sense-organs as described in the Buddhist *Abhidharma* text, analysed in the following lines: The *indriyāṇi*, the sense-organs numbering *six*, inclusive of the Mind; *āyatana*, *six* spheres of the above; *dhātu*, *six* basis of the above sense-organs; *citta-dharma*, functional psychic states numbering multiple in different status of the individual Mind, or in the group-Mind; *vijñāna*, manifold functional consciousness like visual, audio, auder cons taste, touch and the mind consciousness. A person may hold latent potential of becoming the Buddha (as the Buddhists claim). That refers to the procedure of purifying the fourfold status of psychosomatic extension, *brahmavihāra* and the attainment of wisdom *par excellence* called *prajñāpāramitā*.

Bashistha Narayan Sinha reflects on the senses in Jainism, divided into two classes: *jñānendriya* and *karmendriya*. Of them, the importance is given only to the *jñānendriya*. Senses are known as having different parts of the body, such as skin, tongue, nose, eyes, and ears. There are Five varieties of knowledge: empirical, articulate, clairvoyant, mind reading, and omniscient. The vitalities: body, respiration, lifespan, sense of touch, faculty of speech, sense of smell, sense of sight, sense of hearing, and rationality. Different beings are having different vitalities according to the sense they possess.

B.D. Tripathi refers to *Sāṁkhya Kārikā*, enumerating certain limitations of visual perception under the following Five conditions: extremely close contiguity with the stimuli; inattention; infinitesimally of the stimuli; stimuli under cover; and identical structure of units. Visualizing the situation, the author comes to the conclusion that the *real man* is neither only Senses nor only Mind, he is Senses *plus* Mind. At the time of birth, the human body is equipped with primary Mind. Human perception is characterized with certain limitations and tendencies. Under certain conditions, human senses convey false knowledge to the Mind. Human understanding does not exclusively depend either on the innate faculty of Mind or on the data supplied by the senses; rather it is jointly dependent on the two sources of knowledge: *inner* and *outer.* Human mind and ego are primary in their constitutions at the initial phase. Later, they are metamorphosed into secondary constitutions. Consciousness precedes idea.

K.N. Sahay examines the human senses and their purpose, that is, overtaking religious thinking. Drawing from scriptures, he approaches two different types of properties: *divine* and *demonic.* Those possessed by divine (*sāttvika*) character, as elaborated in scriptures, are taken as *pure gift,* and those born with demonic properties (*āsurī*) have turbulence of senses. Religious groups, in different parts of the world, also in divergent societies, give a unique value. This is a universal constant. The capacities of sense-organs "which are nature-born" remain essentially limited. However, the spiritual preceptor would help open the gate of knowledge.

Kalpika Mukherjee finds the functional sense-organs in aesthetic perception. Art reproduces the raw materials of the world, not as they are but being touched upon with the creative genius of the artist. As far as the aesthetic perception is concerned, the involvement of only two sense-organs appears at the first instant. For example, in the case of music, the main transmitter is the auditory organ, whereas in a sculpture or painting or in dance it is the organ of sight that is mainly involved. In the first case, the melody of music, received through the ear, is relayed through the nervous system to the Mind (*manas*), who is the co-ordinator of the series of sounds and the interpreter of the meaning to the connoisseur. In the latter case, also, the whole process occurs through the immediacy of the faculty of sight.

Arttatrana Nayak refers to conceptual understanding of the Five senses known to the Chinese. The concept of *wu xing* or Five agents is closely linked with the Chinese theory of *yin yang* in explaining various universal and cosmological phenomena. The term *wu xing*, morphologically, is a combination of two individual words: *wu* means "Five," and *xing* means "activities." Thus it means "Five activities," explained in terms of Five basic objects: Water, Fire, Wood, Metal and Earth. The ancient philosophers used to regard the objectively existing natural matters as the real and active ones, and believed that the human taste and sensation developed as a result of man's contact with those Five different external worldly substances. The author becomes too philosophical, making such generalities on the growth of human knowledge, social practice and all of the strangeness of the Chinese way, as if different from the other humans.

Hikotaro Furuta introduces Japan as one of the nations having the highest sensitivity in the world, precisely because of its distinguished Four seasons, each bringing beautiful sceneries. The natural environment has helped people growing up in such a beauty: their senses were sharpened, bringing out a flash of *sixth* sense, called *kau* or intuition, and cultivated depth of the Japanese culture. The people of Japan find beauty in Nature and perceived it sensitively, responding to change in nature, appreciating beauty, by using not only the sight but also the senses. Natural beauty occupies an extremely important position, such as Zen. Japanese sensitivity has been brought up with various impressions stuck by Nature. However, their sensitivities have begun declining with the thought that *tradition* and *modernity* are two independent realities. The *spirit* in opposition to *matter.*

A.S. Inam Shastri has developed the dual nature of senses, as reflected in Islamic philosophy. The Holy Koran puts God into the nature of Man. Man has many qualities. When he reaches the (Five), his hearning, his sight and his skin, his sense of touch, his sense of taste, and sense of smell which are specialized form of the organ of touch. All the sensory organs and all their intellectual and emotional counterparts advance us by their use, and pull us down by their misuse. They become tell-tale witness against us, if abused. The Holy Koran refers to physical, moral and spiritual states of man. The *physical state* signifies the uncontrollable spirit. The *moral state* works out the soul from grossness to virtue, and then passes out of the physical state, and becomes a moral being. In the third stage the Soul is freed from all weaknesses and frailty, and is embraced with *spiritual* strength. It is perfectly united with God; cannot exist in separation of Him.

D.M. Solomon takes a specific example of Christian understanding of the Five senses, as reflected in the Bible. Anthropomorphic qualities are attributed to God in the act of *seeing,* implying participation in people's suffering. Significance of *hearing* in biblical revelation is much more significant than any other sense perception. Touch is always symbolic. When Jesus heals by *touch,* he communicates God's power. There are some standing here who will not *taste* death before they see the Son coming in his kingdom. As a personal God, He will smell the fragrance of the sacrifices offered, but only if they follow the commandments and his statutes.

Physical Science and Social Science

The assertion of the ancient philosophy and religion, concerning senses, may be taken today as superstition, abstract model or at best a working hypothesis. On the other hand, the "science search" and the "social experience" may be regarded today as "fact." From the viewpoint of physical science, a natural phenomenon is governed by the physical laws independent of all moral, religious and philosophical influences. The actual acceptance of scientific theories has always been a compromise between the technological and the sociological usage of science. Human conduct is influenced by social, religious and political creeds directly, while the influence of science is rather indirect. The common man is not concerned with the validation of scientific theories. Granted that these two levels of enquiry differ, the similarity can also be imagined because experiments and experiences form a general viewpoint, eventually capable of pulling down the wall.

Most people who wake up to understand the reality raise questions: What's the use of putting a man on the Moon when we see that there is enough space to live on the Earth? The believers venerate the Sun, the Moon and the Stars as divinity. Onkar Prasad has classified the Santal population based on sense-organs such as the *eye*, the *ear*, the *nose*, the *tongue* and the *skin*. The size of the body may vary but the basic sense-organs remain the same. Each limb has a particular form but corresponding variations are found clearly and functionally. For example, the *eye* is the apparatus for seeing, but seeing is further classified into two types: "seeing" through eyes, and "seeing" in dreams with closed eyes which may be auspicious or inauspicious. The *ear* is classified into small, broad, like winnowing fan, mongoose, twisted or dog's ear. *Hearing* is the sense with which the sound is perceived. The *nose* is classified into such types as *sickle-like, cave-like, flat, round* and *insensible*. The *smell* of various types received through nose may be broadly classified into *tolerable* and *intolerable*. The *tongue* is classified into *long, flat* or *broad, thick* and *rough*. The *tastes* of food items, other than rice-beer, are of *twelve* types. The *skin*, as a sensory organ, is valued in socio-religious code of behaviour. *Touch* is also a means of physical intimacy between the members of opposite sex. *Colour* is also an important aspect of vision. The Santals have preference for the *yellow* colour.

Sanghamitra Pal reflects on the function of the sense-organs in the snake-catching technology of the Sapure Mal; the snake-charmers having a lower social status. The author describes all the known forms of snakes (*moshel*) classified into broad categories: *moshel* with and without *nazi* (poison). As a good animal taxonomist, the author describes all the known forms of snakes, sorting out their relationship and habits. The dichotomous key has been used as being the simplest to work through. Complete classification of snakes, as understood from the Sapure, has been given. The Sapure's belief and observation regarding the types of snakes, their habit, mating, birth and death have been recorded largely on the basis of people's knowledge and experience.

Saroj Kr. Pyne and Gautam Samanta have studied animal behaviour during natural disaster *vis-à-vis* their role for the welfare of mankind. The case study shows that the animal's sense of smell is much more superior to that of humans. Reports of animal's *sixth sense* in detecting hurricanes, earthquakes, tsunamis and volcanic eruption, long before the Earth starts shaking, go back to centuries. Some species behave strangely before a catastrophe. Fish are sensitive to low-frequency vibrations and detect tremors long before humans. Elephants feel the quake in their feet and trunks, and they can also figure out what direction the stimulus is coming from, how strong it is and what evasive action to take. Such responses from animals are helpful to humans.

Somasish Ghosh Dastidar and Manojit Debnath, present a simplified form of knowledge regarding the plant's response to external stimuli, a significant finding of Sir Jagadish Chandra Bose. One defining characteristic of Life is an ability to respond to stimuli. Adaptive organisms respond to stimuli because it leads to longevity and survival. Animals have nerves and muscles. Plants also respond by growth patterns. It is possible for a plant to respond to the vibrations, accompanying sound. While there are responses to sound/vibration in plants, there is no controlled study published so far on the musical test. To conclude, plants also respond to external stimuli, and growth patterns and harmony are the prime modulators of such manifestations.

S.N. Ojha deals with bioinformatics of perception which provides plausible explanation of the traditional concept of Five senses that builds up the chemistry of life, a universal home, well known in classical Chinese, Tibetan thought, and Indian philosophy. Modern science now provides the details. The ability to detect *smell* serves essential and aesthetic functions in vertebrates. Many species rely heavily on their sense of *smell* to locate food, detect predators or other dangers, navigate and communicate social information. Olfaction plays a role in mate-choice, mother-infant recognition, and signalling between members of a group. Humans may not depend on olfaction for survival to the same extent as other species, but use extensively to gather information on surroundings. Humans have *taste* sensitivity to different substances, some genetic in origin, and many others inter-individual differences determined by genetic mechanism. Humans can distinguish Five major taste classes: sweet, sour, bitter, salty and *umani* (savoury flavour) exemplified by the *amino acid glutamate.* The field of human taste genetics is at an exciting juncture. Biological process of *hearing* itself is unfolding as genes, underlying hereditary "hearing impairment." Understanding the genetic basis of hearing loss has fascinated human and medical geneticists, for decades. The frequency of hearing-loss is estimated at one per thousand new-born, and half of all cases are attributed to genetic causes. *The Visual* process (Eye) involves a complex set of physiochemical reaction that converts light energy into neuronal signals that transmit information to the brain. The interior part of the eye (including lens, cornea, pupil, iris and cilium body) is responsible for maintaining optional condition for light entering the eye. This involves providing a clear, well-nourished, surface with proper supporting tissue for the cornea and lens to refract the right amount of light into the retina without any interference. The posterior portion of an eye (the retina and optic nerve) is required for the conversion of light energy into chemical and electrical stimuli, and subsequent transmission of the sensory neural signal to the visual cortex of the brain.

Ajeya Jha and H.K.D. Sharma have taken great deal of interest in finding out how modern technology imitates the Five senses, often referred to as artificial sense technologies making use of various types of sensors. A sensor is an entity that tells something about its environment. An electronic sensor is that which gives information about its environment by creating an electrical signal. Thus, electronic feelers design to mimic the "sense of touch," "electronic nose," "electronic tongue," "electronic eye," and "electronic ear." How do they compare with the natural human sense-organs? The authors explain in a satisfactory way as to how real time application is a challenge.

Umesh K. Singh, referring to different observations, draws to a close that there is a differentiation in sense perception between the traditional man and the post-industrial man. The perceptual cognition of the traditional man was more "inner-directed" which has now changed over to the "other directed" cognitive person in contemporary times. Ranging from "super individual's faculties of human senses to the artificially created and technologically added devices," the human senses have produced a wide spectrum of knowledge and cognition of reality. The intervention of technology in contemporary times has enlarged the physical and mental ability of the individual which, though appears to be artificial and contrived, yet helps the physically and mentally impaired to face the outer reality through providing a new contextual apparatus of knowledge. The author presents the story of socio-cultural construction of senses in post-modern society measured by Western scholars in their own imagination, taken literally as the expanding universe of knowledge.

Henrik Janne raises the questions: Who sets the Five senses in order? Nature: because in it there are codes already pre-programmed. That is, there are laws of Nature which can even be seen on a molecular level via modern technology. Nature is supreme, the ultimate. Nature is everything. Now, could one compare Nature with God? The laws of Nature contain the seed of the archaic.

Part I
Philosophy and Religion

1

Tagore's Congregational Addresses on Seeing and Hearing

Sitansu Ray

DEKHA and *Shona*, i.e. seeing and hearing, two reciprocal and complementary roles of two of our Five senses, are consecutive themes of Tagore's congregational addresses delivered on the 4th and 5th *Pauṣ*, respectively in 1315 Bengali era. You will find them in the anthology of Tagore's congregational addresses entitled Santiniketan. These addresses bear Tagore's deep insight and magnanimous introspection of human perception on the one hand and the perceived world of this wonderful creation on the other.

Tagore starts with the phenomenon of light, the main contingent for our visual perception. Light, coming from a far distant source, provides us with the necessary condition for seeing — seeing the wonderful world of beautiful forms. Light is also one of the necessary components for the vegetative growth of trees, flowers, and crops of various kinds around our surroundings. Light shows us much more than we need. *'Seeing'* surpasses our needful items, and leads our vision to the amazing vastness of the sky and the distant horizon. Furthermore, the nocturnal vision of the starry heaven is much more than just knowing the constellations along with their astronomical details. It is to be one with the creation. The world of appearance finds its fulfilment in our analogical perception. Day and night, we are free to see the beauteous forms of creation.

As the sunbeam causes the lotus-bud to bloom, to open its petals, so also it reveals and illumines our consciousness too. We have to see with our full consciousness the perennial fountain of beauty (*rūper jharnā*) arising from and ultimately submerging into the infinite ocean of beauty (*ananta rūpasāgara).*

Quoting from the *Muṇḍaka Upaniṣad* (2.2.7) *Ānandarūpamamṛtam,* Tagore pronounces in full faith that the exquisite beauty of human face is but the lively model of the beauty of that Infinite one, who is manifesting Himself in beautiful forms. We have to see His pleased countenance (*dakṣiṇam mukham, Bṛhadāraṇyaka Upaniṣad*).

Tagore concludes his address along with chanting from the *Śvetāśvatara Upaniṣad* (2.17):

> *yo devo 'gnau, yo 'psu yo viśvam bhuvanamāviveśa* ।
> *ya oṣadhīṣu yo vanaspatiṣu tasmai devāya namonamaḥ* ॥
>
> We bow down to that god who is inherent in fire, water, what to say, throughout the whole creation, even in crop-plants and big trees.

If our sense of vision leads us to that kind of realization, then and then only, it will attain its fulfilment.

Tagore gets highly contemplative that night, gazes at the starry sky from the roof top, and thinks that the vision of the nocturnal firmament is but the silent music of the celestial world.

The next day, he delivers his congregational address *shona.* At the outset he refers to his wonderful experience of the previous night and quotes his own song *baje baje ramya vīṇā*. In this three-stanza song, the first stanza narrates the delightful *vīṇā*-music heard throughout our natural surroundings, such as in the beautiful lotus, the moonlit night, the dark cloudy sky, the fragrance of flowers. The second stanza narrates the enchanting dance-rhythm of the sun and the stars, the rivers and the oceans, the births and the deaths, the emergence and lapse of aeons. The third stanza depicts the beautiful embellishments of the blue sky, the beauty of dawn and dusk, the colourful earthly dust, the devoted hearts of the rich and the poor. The poet feels that the grand cosmic orchestration along with decoration and dancing of everything in the universe is surcharged with passions of love (*preme preme baje*), as it were.

The deluge of magnanimous orchestration of the universe (*bipul viśva-ganer-banya*) is so vital a metaphor used by the poet that he can affirm in full faith:

> This is neither a poetic utterance nor a rhetorical phrase — throughout space and time a continuous orchestration is being reverberated in grand fullness. (my translation)

In emotional ecstasy the poet says again:

> As this devastating deluge of magnanimous music of the universe rushes towards our soul, our single sense-organ is insufficient to receive it; we have to open up all our senses. We receive this musical flow through our eyes, ears, sense of touch and by all means of our body and spirit. We see this grand harmonious concert, listen to it, touch it, smell it and taste it. (my translation)

It is extremely interesting to note the synaesthetic interrelationship of all our Five senses while we enjoy ourselves being one with the whole creation.

The ancient Greek thinkers, had attributed the idea of celestial music to the serene and exactly mathematical movements of the heavenly bodies. Pythagoras was a great thinker of such a kind who had identified the classical mechanics with the sonic properties of the sympathetic vibrations of musical tune and rhythm. This is more than the function of our eardrums alone. While looking at the nocturnal sky, Tagore feels the common rhythm inherent in both the macro-cosmic universe and the micro-cosmic cells of our body. He says that the cosmic music is never separated from the Cosmic artiste, the *vīṇā*-player (sometimes the flute-player, sometimes the singer or sometimes the Naṭarāja, the Cosmic dancer as depicted in various parts of Tagore's works). It should be our aim to synchronize our life-music with the magnanimous music of the ever-evolving universe.

Tagore concludes his address *Shona* with the soulful prayer, "O my Guru, lead me from discord to tunefulness."

2

The Senses

Uma Marina Vesci

THE sequence of the issues of Traditional Thought and Modern Science is extremely significant: After the peaceful Inertia (or Death) at the background of a still amorphous and undistinguished All, Life begins to steer up rising in a surge of Energy brought about by a sudden appearance of conscious sense of solitude in the mind of such very All (*Bṛhadāraṇyaka Upaniṣad* IV. 1, 1.1 ff.) and once Life starts pulsating, the immediate consequence is Expansion. According to another way of conceiving Life, this is the consequence of the main Sacred Action (*karma* or *yajña* — in Latin language *sacrificium* from *sacrum facere*) performed by the gods (*deva*) on the Universal Man (*puruṣa*) (*Ṛgveda* X.90) or, in a later philosophical development, by the main Divinity Prajāpati in an act of self-immolation (*Śatapatha Brāhmaṇa* VI. 1, 1.1 ff.). And the very Act which produced such an effect was the dismemberment of the Victim. In the ritual, the initial unity is broken off into multiplicity, and multiplicity at its turn is again re-collected in a whole in order to be broken off again re-energized (ib.)

Now, in this second moment of the expansion of Life and "creation," the different "pieces" broken apart have to find a way to enter in contact with one another and to organize themselves. This is done through the development of senses. Prajāpati is described as having one thousand eyes — the same as Indra and Viṣṇu before and after Him — while the universe reverberated with cosmic vibrations (later on detected by the *ṛṣis* as the Cosmic Sound from which they captured the meaning and translated It into words through their wisdom).

During the development of creation all the senses are also coming into being as means for the Prajāpati's children (*deva*s and *asura*s) to enter in communication among themselves and with the world (*Śatapatha Brāhmaṇa* in its various references to creation and its development). In classical India also, mind belongs to the realm of senses, though its field of action occurs in more subtle plane.

Besides the divine sphere where senses have an infinite scope and range, human beings are also aware that it is through the same type of means that they not only come in contact with what surrounds them (including the other members of their species) and with nature, but also that these senses are the only available means they have to establish such contacts. Eye, ear, nose, hands (and skin in general) and tongue are the organs that allow them to be aware that they are not alone. Though man in the beginning of his existence was not yet self-conscious, he was aware of not standing in isolation and needed to establish contacts with whatever surrounded him. So the eyes helped him to perceive with clarity the different shapes of the world in which he found himself, and the ears made him alert to the sounds he could detect. Sometimes, due to the precarious situation of his life in jungle's surroundings, sounds could inform him of impending dangers (especially from predators), while smells could drive him towards agreeable flowers and fruits and avert him from upleasant ones. Up till now, animals still make use of smell to mark out their territories or to signal their presence to their fellow beings. In the same manner taste helped the jungle men to discriminate their food of edible and palatable elements from uneatable and even noxious ones. Tactical sensations gave them the security of "reality": they could solidly stand on the ground, or climb on trees and touch with their hands branches, fruits, seeds and even roots which they could dig out with convenient tools.

Besides using senses for survival against external dangers and for satisfying internal needs, Man also found in them the powerful means for establishing contacts and have relationship within the members of his own group, and of other aliens, if by chance they crossed each other's path. Stretching arms and hands for touching one's neighbour, embracing and making love with the female folk, ensure mutual help, comradeship and the procreation of the species. This is also enhanced by the reciprocal smell as sexually attractive, while sight and hearing give the possibility of mutual understanding (even through detecting one another's expressive moods). Common taste can also strengthen the pleasure of sharing.

But, at the beginning specially, Man was not yet self-centred and, though making use of his senses for survival and interacting, had a natural impulse to project them into the cosmos itself. So, what is more "natural" than seeing the main luminaries of the sky — the day sun and the night moon — as the main divine Eyes and to consider the wind, *vāyu*, as the producer of Sounds involving hearing? The Earth and the trees covering her could stand for cosmic Tact as well as for the smell detected by appropriate organs. The cosmic Taste, in Brāhmanic terms, could be ascribed to Prajāpati himself in creating the sacrificial Act: sweetness and sourness are essential in the distribution of its creative dismembered body (*Śatapatha Brāhmaṇa* VI.1, 1 ff.).

3

The Five Senses Theory
Indian Approach

Niradbaran Mandal Kavyatarkatirtha

FROM the remote ancient time of Vedic literature, Indian thinkers were very conscious about the concept of Five senses. Philosophical thoughts are well-marked in the *mantra*-portion of the Vedas (as seen in the Puruṣa Sūkta, *Aghamarṣanasūkta*, etc.) and in a more developed form in the Upaniṣads. But it would not be incorrect to say that Sāṁkhya philosophy is the first step of Indian mind towards systematizing the concepts or elements (*tattva*s in their terminology) relating to philosophy. The Five senses theory can be regarded as basis to them. How? The answer to this question requires some clarification of the concepts of twenty-five *tattva*s.

But before going into that it would be better to present and discuss some Vedic (including ancient Upaniṣads) passages where those concepts are obviously stated in order to show the historical and the literary background of Sāṁkhya views about Five senses.

It is said in the *Kaṭhopaniṣad* (perhaps a post-Buddhist Upaniṣad)

ātmānām rathinam viddhi śarīram rathameva tu ।
buddhiṁ tu sārathiṁ viddhi manaḥ pragrahameva ca ॥

indriyāṇi hayānāhurviṣayaṁs teṣu gocarān ।
ātmendriya-mano-yuktaṁ bhoktetyāhurmaniṣiṇaḥ ॥
— *Kaṭha* 1.3.3-4

It means — Know that *ātmā* is the owner of this chariot (body). The body is the chariot. And *buddhi* is its *sārathī*. And the mind is the *pragraha* (bridle) and (they) say that *indriyas* and objects (like colour, etc.) are their field (for walking). The wise persons say — that the observer or the enjoyer (of this world) is associated with body, sense and mind.

Hence, we see that the poet-philosopher of the Upaniṣads compared the human body with a chariot. *Ātmā* or soul dwells inside it. And the *indriyas* are the horses of this chariot (because with the forces of *indriyas* the body moves towards the objects). From here we can realize that the *indriyas* are most important things to a soul to keep its link with the objects of the outer world. And the objects like colour, etc. are the ways (*mārga* as the commentator Śaṅkarācārya explains this word *gocara*) (vide the commentary on the *Kaṭhopaniṣad* by Śaṅkarācārya).

But this is only a metaphor. This may not be taken as a systematic presentation of the *tattvas*. Hence, to serve this purpose the poet-philosopher of the *Kaṭhopaniṣad* describes the *tattvas* again as follows —

indriyebhyaḥ parā hyarthā arthebhyaścā paraṁ manaḥ ।
manasastu parā buddhirbuddherātmā mahānparaḥ ॥

mahataḥ param avyaktam avyaktāt puruṣaḥ paraḥ ।
puruṣānna paraṁ kiñcitsā kāṣṭhā sā parā gatiḥ ॥
— 1.3.10–11

It means *arthas* are subtler than the *indriyas* and mind is subtler than *arthas*. *Buddhi* is subtler than mind. And *manaḥ ātmā* is subtler than *buddhi*. And *avyakta* is subtler than *buddhi*. And *avyakta* is subtler than *mahat*. *Puruṣa* is subtler than *avyakta*. But there is nothing subtler than the *puruṣa*. He is the subtlest, the highest one. He is the ultimate way.

Here we see that the description has been started with the *indriyas* as if *indriyas* are the most outward gates. Even the *arthas* are subtler than the *indriyas*. What are these *arthas*? Not clearly stated in these lines — but it can be guessed that as they are subtler than the *indriyas* so they must be subtle *arthas* which are inner and supplied by the *indriyas* to the mind (vide the commentary upon the *Nyāya-Sūtra* 1.1.9 *bhoktavya indriyārthaḥ*) like *śabda* (sound), *sparśa* (touch), *rūpa* (colour and form), *rasa* (taste) and *gandha* (smell). In Sāṁkya philosophy they are called *tanmātras* also.

But the commentator established it in another way. He said —

> *sthūlāni tāvadindriyāni tāni yaiḥ arthairātmaprakāśanāya ārabdhāni* ।
>
> *tebhya indriyebhyaḥ svakāryebhyaste parā hi arthāḥ sūkṣmāḥ* ॥
>
> It means — *indriyas* are gross (than the *arthas*) because they are made of those *arthas* for their self-luminations or existence, as the cause is subtler than the effect so *arthas* are subtler than the *indriyas*.

It can be remembered here that according to Nyāya-Vaiśeṣika philosophy — the *indriyas* are regarded *bhautika* — i.e. made of *pañca mahābhūta* — so their nature in *bhautika*. But according to the Sāṁkhya philosophy they are *ahaṁkārika*.

So, we see that there are differences in opinions regarding this.

Another thing is also remarkable here. We see here that mind is stated as if distinct from the *indriyas*. Mind here does not seem to be included in the group of the *indriyas*. In this regard also there are different views in Indian philosophy. Even a great Vaidāntic like Dharmarājādhvarīndra firmly tried to put arguments to reject the view that mind is also an *indriya*, though Śaṅkarācārya, the great propounder of their philosophy accepted that the *indriyas* are eleven in number, (i.e. five *jñānendriyas* + five *karmendriyas* + mind). But it is also true that *karmendriyas* are *indriyas* only in secondary sense (*lākṣaṇika*) because they do not produce knowledge.

It is also to be noted that in the above-quoted *mantra* of the Upaniṣad, the *buddhi* and *mahān ātmā* are presented here separately, and the *ahāṁkāratattva* (egoism) is not accepted, which may be a later development in Sāṁkhya philosophy. But in this respect it has a close similarity with the philosophy of Pātañjala Yoga which refused to count the *ahaṁkāra* as a distinct *tattva*. The followers of the Yoga philosophy accepted the *ahaṁkāra* as *asmitā*.

So, it seems to us that the philosophy of Sāṁkhya developed through stages. It must have undergone some changes (as evidence in many passages of ancient texts like the Upaniṣads, the *Mahābhārata*, etc.) while passing through the ages. But the basic concept of the five senses remained unchanged. There was a long history of the developement of Sāṁkhya thought even before the *Sāṁkhya-Kārikā* which is regarded as the oldest document of Sāṁkhya treatise available to us.

However, we can now make an inquiry about the derivative meaning of the word *indriya*. The word *indriya* is really a very old one. Even in the *R̥gveda*, the oldest text of Indian literature, it has been used. But the sense of this word in some *mantras* of the *R̥gveda* was perhaps slightly different from the sense in which we use it now. For instance we can quote this line from the *R̥gveda* — *tamaḥ sadhāya dhāsathā svindriyam* (vide *R̥gveda* 1.111.2). Dayānanda, a famous commentator says here — *indriya* means *vijñāna*. But it means power also. For this meaning we can observe other passages also from the Vedic literature as follows:

vīryavānityevaitadāha yadāhendriyavāniti
— *Śatapatha* 3.9.3.25

mayidamindra indriyam dadhātu
— *Śatapatha* 1.8.1.42

But at the time of the great grammarian Pāṇini the word seems to be fixed to denote the sense which is closely related with knowledge and power of cognizing. Hence he made a *sūtra* as follows:

indriyāmindraliṅgamindradṛṣtamindrasṛṣṭamindra justamindra-dattamiti vā — see Pāṇini *Aṣṭādhyāyī* 5.2.93 (*justam/yustam* also reading).

We can say according to Pāṇini the word *indriya* has been derived from the word *Indra* adding the suffix *gha* after it (i.e. *Indra+gha* (*iya*) = *indriya*). Grammarians were also of the opinion that *Indra* here means the *ātmā* or soul, thus it is said in the *Kāśikā* (a commentary on Pāṇinian *sūtras*) — *indra ātmā*. The meaning of the suffi *gha* (or *iya*) is also clear from Pāṇinian *sūtra* as quoted above. It may mean *liṅga, drṣṭa, sṛṣṭa, justa* or *datta*. So the total meaning of this combination of these two words (i.e. *Indra+iya*) becomes like this — (1) Mark of the soul, (2) Seen by the soul, (3) Created by the soul, (4) Possessed by or enjoyed by the soul, or (5) Given by the soul. All these meanings have distinct significances. We can discuss a bit about these briefly and examine how far they are in accordance with the views of different branches of Indian philosophy which were developed later.

Can *indriya* be a mark of the soul? Let us see what the view of old Indian logicians is (Naiyāyika) on this point. It is said in the *Nyāya-Sūtra* — *icchā-dveṣa-prayatna-sukha-duḥkha-jñānānyātmano liṅgam.* It means — desire, envy, effort, pleasure, pain and knowledge are the marks of the soul. (*Nyāya-Sūtra* 1.1.10). But *indriyas* are not counted here as the mark of the soul in this list. It seems to be so. But there is an indication of the fact that *indriyas* are the marks. By the word knowledge the *indriyas* may be indicated to some commentator like Dayānanda, etc. *Indriya* means knowledge also (as stated before). So, there is no difficulty that *indriya* is *indraliṅga* or mark of soul in the light of views of the later thinkers also. In fact, we can discover a link of similar thought in both the grammar and Indian logic at least on this point.

It transpires from the above discussion that (in any type of body) if there is *indriya* then there must be soul, because *indriya* is the mark of soul.

Now the question arises how to know that there are *indriyas*. Can these marks (i.e. *indriyas*) be perceived? The answer to this question will be in the negative since *indriyas* can comprehend outer things only. They cannot perceive themselves. In fact, they are the instruments for perception and hence they are involved with the process of perception and hence the instruments cannot be the object of knowledge. So, the philosophers accept the *indriyas* as *atindriya padārtha*. It is clearly stated in the Upaniṣad that – *parāñci khāni vyatṛṇāt svayambhūḥ* (i.e. God created the *indriyas* as facing towards the outer world). So, the question arises that if they are not perceived then how can we know that there are *indriyas*?

To establish their existence, the Sāṁkhya philosophers (and some others also) laid down an inference as follows — the knowledge of colour, etc. possesses some instrument because knowledge of colour, etc. is a kind of action. All actions possess some instrument. Knowledge is a kind of action. So, knowledge also possesses some instruments. The instruments (for acquiring knowledge) are called *indriyas*. Hence, *indriyas* cannot be perceived normally (i.e. except extraordinary yogic perception). They can easily be inferred — and this inference as stated before is technically called *sāmānyatodṛṣṭa anumāna*.

Now a brief description of the senses can be given according to various branches of Indian philosophy as follows:

Sāṁkhya

According to Sāṁkhya there are five senses relating to a soul (i.e. human). These are called *jñānendriyas*. But they accept five *karmendiyas* also. And another thing must be noted in this connection that *manaḥ* or mind is accepted by them as both *jñānedriya* and *karmendriya*. In the *Sāṁkhya-Kārikā*, it is clearly stated as follows:

> *buddhindriyāni cakṣuḥśrotraghrāṇarasanatvagākhyāni* ।
> *vākpāṇipādapāyūpasthāni karmendriyāṇyāhuḥ* ॥
>
> — *Sāṁkhya-Kārikā* 26
>
> It means — there are five senses of perceptions like eye, ear, nose, tongue and skin. They call another five like *vāk* (speech faculty), hand, foot, anus and generative organ as *karmendriyas* or faculties of action.

The objects of the senses of perception are colour (form), sound, smell, taste and feeling (touch), respectively. And the objects of the faculties of action are speaking, holding, walking, excretion and lust. It is to be noted here that *karmendriyas* are regarded as *indriyas* in the secondary sense only because they are not directly involved in producing knowledge. So the theory of five senses is maintained here. Sāṁkhya also maintains that the functions of the senses take place successively and simultaneously (see the *Sāṁkhya-Sūtra* 2.32). (This is true only when ten outer *indriyas* and three inner *antaḥkaraṇas* are taken into account.) Let us say a bit more clearly. The function of the five senses is called *ālocanā* (cognition). The function of *ahaṁkāra* is called *abhimāna* (egotizing). The function of *buddhi* (judging) is called *adhyavasāya* (ascertainment or deciding). And the function of *manaḥ* (mind) is called *saṅkalpa* (conceptualizing). These four functions can take place successively and simultaneously.

Now, what about *manaḥ* or mind? If it is an *indriya* then a question arises — is it a *jnānendriya* or is it *karmendriya?* We have told before that there is a controversy about whether it is an *indriya.* And great Vaidāntic Dharmarājādhvarīndra refused to accept the *manaḥ* (mind) as an *indriya.* Though it is clearly stated in a famous text like the *Gītā* that *manaḥsaṣṭhaindriyāṇi* — (mind is the sixth) but he explained it in another way. He said that there is no difficulty in accepting the mind as the sixth even in spite of the fact that it is not an *indriya.*

But Sāṁkhya clearly accepted *manaḥ* as both a *jñānendriya* and *karmendriya.* It is said in the *Sāṁkhya-Kārikā* (27) —

> *udhayātmakāmatra manaḥ, saṅkalpakamindriyam ca sādharmyāt, guṇapariṇāmaviśeṣānnānātvam vāhdyabhedāśca.*
>
> It means — the mind partakes of the nature of both *jnānendriya* and *karmendriya.* Its function is conceptualizing. It is an *indriya* because it has a similarity with the *indriyas.* (If all senses (eleven) have the nature of a modification of the single *sāttvika ahaṁkāra,* how is the diversity to be explained? To this, the author replies) — Diversity proceeds from the difference of the modification of the constituents like conditions.

It is also remarkable here, as pointed out by Sāṁkhya, a common function of the organs is of five airs, breath, etc. (i.e. *pañcaprāṇa*). The five airs, breath, etc. are sustained by the three internal organs together.

Yoga

Yoga philosophy has a great similarity to Sāṁkhya philosophy in many respects. They share equally philosophical views like *satkāryavāda, pariṇāmavāda,* multitude of souls, etc. On epistemological level also they are very similar. It is interesting to note that the commentator on the *Yoga-Sūtras* compared the *indriyas* with some channels through which the mind or *citta* keeps contact with external objects. He said:

> *indriyapraṇālikayā cittasya vāhyavastūparāgād* . . . etc.
>
> — commentary on the *Sūtra* 1.7
>
> It means — perception is the mental operation about the external objects, it takes up the colour of those things through the channels of the senses and is the determinative chief of the specific character of the object endowed with generic and specific nature.

Nyāya Vaiśeṣika

According to the author of *Nyāya-Sūtra* (of Gautama), five senses are as follows : *ghrārṇarasanacakṣustvakśrotrānīndriyāṇi bhūtebhyaḥ* (*Nyāya Sū* 1.1.12). According to him mind is also an *indriya.* But that is not mentioned in the group of these five because in every type of perception, the other senses may be different but the contact with mind remains the same (vide the *Bhāṣya* upon *sūtra.* 1.1.4). In the opinion of the Naiyāyikas these *indriyas* are *bhautika* which is contrary to the view of Sāṁkhya. Naiyāyikas set forth some arguments against this, i.e. nature of senses differ, so they must come from different causes. But Sāṁkhya, on the basis of scripture maintains that all *indriyas* come from one cause, i.e. *sāttvika ahaṁkāra.*

Vedānta

It is said before that there is controversy about the view that mind is an *indriya.* Some Vaidāntics do not accept this although the propounder of their doctrine, great Śaṅkarācārya accepted that *indriyas* are eleven in number. Another thing to be noted is this. They had accepted four inner *karaṇa* (internal sense) like *manaḥ, buddhi, ahaṁkāra* and *citta.* Otherwise it can be said that they have followed the Sāṁkhya view on the *indriyas* a lot (vide *Vedānta-Sūtra* and *Vedāntaparibhāṣā,* Chapter I).

Mīmāṁsā

Mīmāṁsakas also accepted six *indriyas* (Bhāṭṭa School). Hence, it is said in the *Manameyodaya,* a famous treatise on Bhāṭṭa Mīmāṁsā that *kani, punarindriyāni? cakṣurasanādghrān-asparśanśrotrāṇi manaśceti sadindriyāṇi.* Another point is to be noted here. Though they have some similarity with the Naiyāyikas they do not accept *samavāya* as a relation. So according to them relation between the sound and the ear is not *samavāya.*

It can be noted here that Navya-Naiyāyikas formulated a definition of *indriya* in accordance with their philosophy of

Navya-Nyāya. The definition runs as — *śabdetarodbhūta-viśeṣaguṇā nāsrayatve sati jñānakarṇamanaḥ saṁyogāśrayatvam.*

It is also remarkable that the Buddhists and Jainas also accepted five senses. But in the *Nyāyabindu*, Dharmakīrti, a famous Buddhist logician, has treated *indriyavijñāna* and *manovijñāna* separately.

For the ordinary perceptual knowledge *indriya*s are required. But it is maintained in many Śāstras, from ancient time to modern, that God's perception is beyond senses. Hence, it is said in the Upaniṣads —

> *paśyatyacakṣuḥ sa śṛṇotyakarṇaḥ apāṇipādo javano grahītā.*
>
> He can see without eyes, he can hear without ears, he can take without hand and he can go without legs.

But that is a different topic which requires another place for discussion.

References

Indian Philosophy — A Modern Approach, ed. Narayan Kumar Chattopadhyaya, 1979.

Kārikāvalī, New Delhi: Rastriya Sanskrit Sansthan, 2002.

Mānameyodaya, tr. Dinanath Tripathi, Sanskrit College, 1989.

Ṛgveda, ed. Haraf, Calcutta: Haraf Prakashani, 1976.

Sāṁkhyakārikā, tr. Ramsankar Bhattacharya, Motilal Banarsidass, 1967.

Sāṁkhya-Sūtra and Sāṁkhya System, ed. Richard Garbe, 1987.

Sāṁkhyatattvakaumudī, tr. Narayan Goswami, Sanskrit Pustak Bhandar, 1998.

Upaniṣad, ed. A. Sen, S. Tattvabhusan and M. Ghosh, Calcutta: Haraf Prakashani, 1994.

Vedāntasāra, ed. Vipadbhanjam Pal, Sanskrit Pustak Bhandar, 1994.

The Yogsūtra of Patañjali, ed. and tr. Bangali Bada, 1979.

Yuktidīpikā, vol. 1, ed. Shiv Kumar and D.N. Bhargava, Delhi: Eastern Book Linkers, 1990.

4

Human Sense-Organs
as Described in the Buddhist Abhidharma

S.K. Pathak

ANTHROPOLOGISTS, ethnologists and sociologists usually lay emphasis on the human behaviours and their social reference. A human being, according to the Indian perspectives, is a part of nature as a whole. Its general relationship with the nature is similar to that with other living beings belonging to the earth. Rationality, the human social behaviour, becomes the means that are appropriate to the ends. In other words, a rational action is effective in achieving the purpose that a human being intends to achieve. In the sphere of human knowledge, when a belief is established scientifically for application, that may be considered rational particularly in the extensive philosophical debates like epistemology, ontology, science and rationalism.

The human sense organs (HSO) are instruments of the human knowledge as a branch of philosophy that deals with epistemology. On the other hand, ontology and metaphysics are concerned with the fundamental kind of things or objects which exist in the world. Greek philosophers like Plato (428-348 BCE), a pupil of Socrates (470-399 BCE), and teacher of Aristotle (384-322 BCE) pioneered in deductive inquiry of the human mind based on rationality. That amounted to generate the ethics, a branch of human social behaviour. In that also the HSO are instrumental to distinguish the ethical from the unethical. Critically speaking, the Greek trinity of the philosophers of pre-Christianity, influenced European thinkers extensively from Socretian *Dialogue on Ethics* to Plato's *Idealism* followed by Aristotelian Empiricist wing of Greek philosophy. Again, that could not overlook the instrumentation of the HSO to estimate the Epistemological decisions like empiricism, rationalism or idealism. Those became an effective means to know the objective world and the argument to experience or to perceive, beginning from Plato's ontological theory of forms up to the latest phases like scientific realism. Eminent philosophies of Europe like Emile Durkhem's (1858–1917) conception of "social facts," and Max Weber's (1864–1920) emphasis on individual actors accepted HSO for instrumentation of knowing. Again, Karl Marxian (1818–83) materialism related to production and modes in distribution or *New Left Intellectual Movements* led by historians Edward Thompson (1924-93) followed the same. *In the Making of the English Working Class 1963,* Marxist contemporary leader of Campaign for Nuclear Disarmament, Perry Anderson (1938-) and social theorist historian and the cultural theorist Raymond Williams and the sociologist Stuart Hall could not ignore the importance of the HSO. The HSO became vital in all perspectives whether epistemological, ontological or sociological.

Comparatively, the Buddhist psychological treatise like *Abhidharma-Kośa* of Vasubandhu (fourth century CE) of Nālandā endeavoured to estimate the HSO in a different perspective. He followed the seven *Abhidharma* texts in Pāli (*circa* 5–3 BCE) and seven *Abhidharma* texts in Sanskrit (*circa* third century BCE – third cnetury CE) as enumerated in the Appendix I. The Buddha's enunciation of twelve categories of *nidāna* specimens relating to the psychosomatic process by the Department Origination in successive order of causes and effects, *pratītyasamutpāda,* becomes important for the HSO. They are caused by craving or desire (*tṛṣṇā*) and effectuated to the stronger clingings as that of the psychomorphosis *upādāna*. Again that morphic clinging, being a cause, is effectuated to tend the re-existence of the individual and to take birth.

Enumerations of the HSO

Five sense-organs, namely eyes, ears, nose/nostrils, tongue and touch, follow, in general, with their respective response to the phychosomatic enclave. For functional cognition of the thing, whether subjective, objective or subjective-objective, the above sense-organs are media. In that respect all humans hold commonness unless those sense-organs are deficient owing to the psychosomatic non-functioning in respect to a particular.

According to the Indian thinkers, the mind is also regarded as a sense-organ to experience introvert sensation when the above doors of sense-organs may be closed. In this regard a chapter dealing with the physiology of the HSO *indriyasthāna* deals with diagnosis and prognosis in the Indian medical text *Caraka Saṁhitā* (early English tr., Calcutta 1890–1911 and Keith AHSL 2001, pp. 506-7). It enumerates nine sense-organs *nava-dvāra* inclusive of the genetic organs for *śanrasthāna* dealing with embryology and anatomy of the human body. So, the holistic experience of phenomena all around a person, the functionality of the mind becomes an agent and an instrument as well. That means, the six sense-organs tend to cognize "forms" of a phenomenon as the ontology claims. In that respect a concept is not void. Since it is thought-constructed, a concept is also constituted through the mind sense-organ *mana-indriya*. The social facts and social ideas are also constituted by HSO dependently conditioned. The psychosomatic factors become cogent to determine the quantum of sensational receptability of the HSO as stratified in three major categories:

(1) persons of mild receptibility (below the average),

(2) those of average receptibility (*madhya indriya*), and

(3) of the above average or sharp receptibility (*tīkṣṇa indriya*). An empirical psychologist also measures such categories by the IQ texts and deploy them according to respective merits. Interrelations among the HSOs with the phenomenal objects in generating mental factors may be shown below, as the *Abhidharma* refers :

Sense- organs (*indriyāṇi*)	**Phenomenal object (*āyatana*)**	**Basic contention (*dhātu*)**	**Psychic cognition in response *vijñāna***
eye, sense-organ *cakṣu indriya*	visual objects *cakṣurāyatana*	form *rūpa dhātu*	visual cognition responds to the mind *cakṣur-vijñāna*
nose, s.o. *nāsikāndriya*	smelling objects *ghrāṇāyatana*	perfume/ ardour *gandha*	cognitive smelling *r-m* *ghrāna-vijñāna*
ear, s.o. *karṇendriya*	audible objects *śrotrāyatana*	sound *śabda*	cognitive response by *śrotra-vijñāna*
tongue, s.o. *jihvendriya*	tastable objects *svāda-āyatana*	taste *rasa*	cognitive response by taste *svāda-vijñāna*
body, s.o. *kāyendriya*	factual objects *kāya-āyatana*	touch *kāyā-sparśtavya*	cognitive response by touch *kāya-vijñāna*
mind, sense-organ *manaindriya*	mental object *mana-āyatana*	thought *bhāvanā*	cognition by mind *manovijñāna*

perturbed mind for sensation as a sense-organ *kliṣṭa manainindriya*	pervasive mental object *kliṣṭa mana-āyatana*	perturbation *manaḥkleśa*	mental perturbed cognition *kliṣṭa mano-vijñāna*
mind, sense-organs dependent on actions performed by a person, *karma yukta vipāka mana-indriya*	actions-based mental object, pleasant or unpleasant *vipāka mana-āyatana*	Pleasure or displeasure *harṣa vā anutāpa vimarśa*	mental response to cognition of pleasure or displeasure. *vipāka-mano-vijñāna*

Machanism for Interactions

Interactions between HSO with the phenomena, whether internal or external, are within the scope of the Empirical physiology. The sensory and the motor nerves conducted by the brain operational functionality of a human being interact in the time and space context to experience knowledge. These functionaries generate sensation and perception as the psychologists enumerate.

The sensory nerves and the motor nerves react according to the stimuli of the HSO in the time and space context. Thereby the psychic factors like sensation, perception and others generate, tending to physical and mental change of a human being. In this respect the Buddhists have analysed those factors in different mechanism to function in the following lines:

1. *indriyāṇi* — (i) the sense-organs numbering six, inclusive of the mind.
2. *āyatana* — (a) six spheres of the above.
3. *dhātu* — (d) six basis of the above sense-organs.
4. *citta-dharma* — (c) functional psychic states numbering

multiple in different status of the individual mind or in the group mind.

5. *vijñāna* — (v) manifold functional consciousness like, the visual consciousness *cakṣu–v,* the audio-cons, *śrotra–v.,* the odour cons *ghrāṇa–v.,* the taste cons *svāda-v.,* the touch-cons *sparśa-v.* and the mind-consciousness, *mano-vijñāna.*

Regarding functional mechanism in respect to each sense-organ, the act(s) performed by the individual or those in a group collectively may produce determinable results by the law of sequence in cause and effects *pratītyasamūtpāda.* Resultantly, in successive order the promotion at the first level of mind sense-organs *mṛdu-I* holds the possibility to enraise up to the third level *tīkṣṇa-i.* In due course, a person develops the potential of becoming the Buddha by the efficiency of self-determination by the sense-organs.

HSO Purification Formula

A person holds latent potential of becoming the Buddha, as a Buddhist claims. That refers to the procedure of purifying the HSO like the Noble Eightfold Path, the fourfold status of psychosomatic extension *brahmavihāra,* and the attainment of wisdom *par excellence, prajñāpāramitā.* The procedure may be put in a formula as given below.

impure a+b+c (caused by <impure-i = impure V.
purified a+b+c caused by pure-i = pure V.

The above may be elaborated here. The impure HSO pervades the — (a) sense organic spheres, (b) their bases and their respective consciousness, and (c) functional psychic states under the influence of the ignorant acts performed by notions. Here "notions" refer to malignant functioning of HSO that may commit mistakes like perceiving a conch-shell as a silver coin. As a result of that the respective sense conciousness of vision *cakṣu-vijñāna* becomes wrong and malignant.

By observing the procedures prescribed above, depending on the status, the HSO may be purified with self-determination in order to achieve the pure consciousness *vimala-vijñāna*. In other words, the correct perspective of reality, according to Buddhism, is to hold the vision for cognition of that which occurred *yathābhūtajñāna darśana*. The purified HSO becomes efficient to what occurred in reality. Otherwise, no cognition is free from error as ordinarily experienced by the HSO.

Biased Perceptions by the Impure HSO

Since beginning of the cultivation of the human mind, repeated warnings have been levied for purifying HSO for unbiased perceptions of the phenomenon concerned in order to avoid hegemonies in the individual life, or those in the social history. It is a pity that those wise sayings remain unheeded. The impure HSO becomes the cause of biased perception instead of unbiased cognition of the reality. That amounts to catechism in dialectics like is or is-not. The veils in knowing the real create multiple theories with imperfect perception.

Reciprocity of the mind-consciousness and other sense organic consciousness will lead to biased imperfect perception about a phenomenon whether subjective, objective or subjective-objective, unless and until the purified HSO will function. So, the reality is twofold: the conventional reality that darkens with veils of notions and the prospective reality in supersession of the former, that awakens with effulgence of becoming the perfect.

For the achievement of the said status, the fourfold measures of the mindfulness *smṛtyapasthāna* in every movement for cleansing the impurities of the HSO are: Be mindful of what the eyes see; Be mindful of what the ears listen; Be mindful of what the tongue tastes; Be mindful of what the nose inhales; Be mindful of what is touched; and Be mindful of that which is Mind.

Successive process in order of Cause Effect

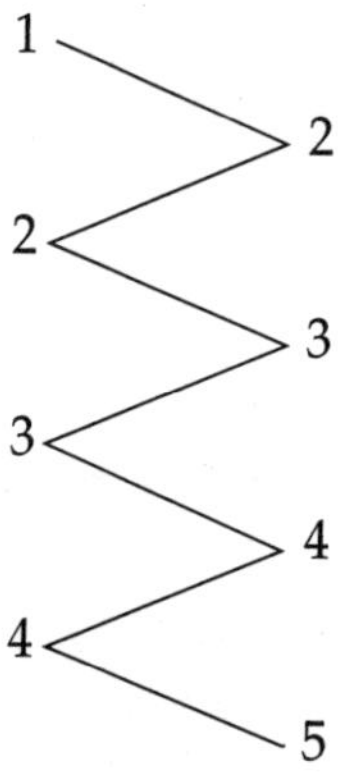

and so on

Reverse order for cessation of Effect Cause

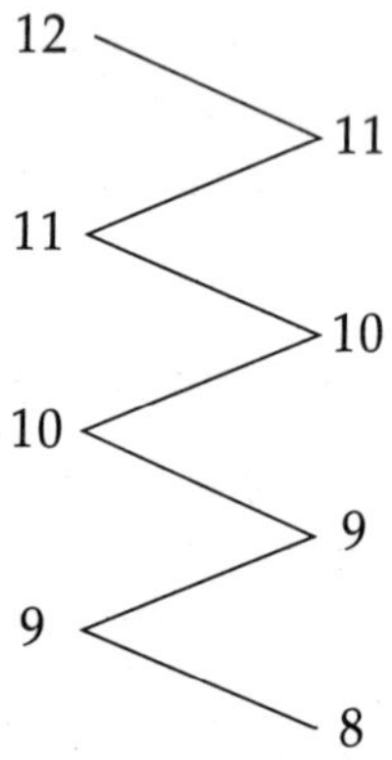

and so on

The twelve specimens of the Law of Dependent Origination have been enunciated in the *Abhidharma/Abhidhamma* treatises, vide Appendix II.

Appendix I

1. Sanskrit *Abhidharma* (*Sarvāstivādin*) 1. *Jñānaprasthāna Shāstra* Author: Ārya–Kātyāniputra	1. *Paṭṭhānapakarana Mahappakaraṇa*–Mahākassapa is said to have recited *Abhidhamma* texts in the recited *Abhi-dhamma* texts in the first Buddhist Council in India held at Rājagṛha after the demise of the Buddha *circa* 542 BCE except *Kathāvatthu*. That was recited by Moggaliputta Tissa in the Third Buddhist Council at Pāṭaliputra during the rule of Aśoka.
2. *Prajñapti Śāstra* Author: Ārya Maudgalyāyana	2. *Puggalapaññaṭi* — Description of individuals.
3. *Prakaraṇapāda* Author: Ārya Vasumitra	3. *Vibhaṅg* — Classification ofpyscho-physical phenomena.
4. *Saṅgīti-paryāya* Author: Ārya Mahākauṣṭilya	4. *Yamaka* — The Book of double questions.
5. *Vijñānakāya* Author: Sthavira Devaśarma	5. *Kathāvatthu* — Subject of dis-course.
6. *Dharmaskandha* Author: Ārya Śāriputra	6. *Dharmasaṅganī* — Compendium of *dhamma* phenomena (psycho-physical)
7. *Dhātukāya* Author: Ārya–Puraṇa	7. *Dhātuvāda* — Discourses on elements.

The authors, according to the Tripiṭaka and Āgamas, were contemporaries of the Buddha.

Appendix II

Causal Law of Dependent Origination			
Successive Order		Reverse Order	
1.	Ignorance (of the individual)	*avidyā*	12.
2.	Latent psycho-impression	*saṁskāra*	11.
3.	Imperfect consciousness	*vijñāna*	10.
4.	Psycho-physical constituents	*nāma-rūpa*	9.
5.	Six sense-organs and their objects	*ṣaḍāyatana*	8.
6.	Contact sense-organs with objects	*sparśa*	7.
7.	Sensation	*vedanā*	6.
8.	Craving/thirst	*tṛṣṇā*	5.
9.	Mental clinging for craving/thirst	*upādāna*	4.
10.	Strong desire for availability in existence again and again	*bhāva*	3.
11.	Birth of an individual	*jāti*	2.
12.	Old age, suffering and death	*jarā-maraṇa*	1.

5

Senses in Jainism

Bashistha Narayan Sinha

JAINISM is one of the Śramaṇic traditions of Indian culture. It is also one of the atheistic schools of Indian philosophy. It has 24 prophets (*tīrthaṅkaras*) including Ṛṣabhadeva, the first of prehistoric age, and Mahāvīra the 24th of the sixth century BCE. The ultimate reality in this system is known as substance (*padārtha*). Substance is divided mainly as the extended (*astikāya*) and the unextended (*anāstikāya*). *Anāstikāya* is one which has no body. *Astikāya* — substances which possess extension are divided into two classes, viz. *jīva* or that which is living and *ajīva* or that which is non-living. *Jīva* is enjoyer while *ajīva* is enjoyed. Umāsvāti, in his famous work *Tattvārthasūtra*, has defined *jīva* as that which posseses *upayoga. Upayoga* means consciousness. Therefore, a *jīva* or soul may be known as a conscious substance. It is also classified as that which is liberated (*mukta*) and that which is suffering from worldly bondage (*baddha*). Again it is divided as mobile (*trasa*) and immobile (*sthavara*). The mobiles possess bodies of different degrees. Therefore they are put into four classes such as five sensed, four sensed, three sensed and two sensed. The immobiles have also different bodies in which they live, such as water, fire, air, earth and plants. They have tactual sense only. The different degrees of body depend on the activities (*karmas*) performed. A *jīva* occupies its body according to the deeds done in the past life.

Senses

A well-known Jaina thinker, Sukhalal Sanghavi, has defined sense as that through which knowledge is gained.[1] Generally, senses are divided into two classes — *jñānendriya* and *karmendriya.* In the Jaina system of philosophy importance has been given to the *jñānendriya* only. Why? It is very difficult to say. But, at least, this must be known here that the senses which help a man achieve different types of knowledge[2] are known as *jñānendriya* and the senses through which one performs activities like walking, handling, speaking, etc. are treated as *karmendriya.* Senses (knowledge-giving) are five in number.

All knowledge-giving senses are known in two ways —

1. Cluster of matter (*dravyendriya*)
2. Modes of the soul (*bhāvendriya*)

The senses as clusters of matter have two types:[3]

(i) Physical organs (*nirvṛtti indriyas*) which are seen externally as the different parts of the body.

(ii) Capacities of physical organs to function (*upakaraṇa-indriya*)

The senses as the modes of soul have also two types:[4]

(i) Sentient potential (*labdhi-indriya*)

(ii) Sentient-application (*upayoga indriya*)

Sentient potential is the capacity of the soul to apply the physical senses. The *Svopajña Bhāṣya* explains that sentient potential is realised by the active arising of the body-making *karma* and also the partial elimination and partial suppression of the

1. *Tattvārtha-Sūtra,* tr., Sukhalal Sanghavi, p. 56.
2. *Pañcendriyāṇi*/15 *Dvividhāni* 116 *Tattvārtha-sūtra,* Chapter-2.
3. *nirvṛttyupakaraṇe dravendriyam,* 117 — ibid.
4. *labdhyupayogān bhāvendriyam,* 118 — ibid.

knowledge-covering *karma*. The *Sarvārthasiddhi* affirms this latter cause but does not mention the former. It identifies sentient application with the striving of the soul to produce physical senses.[5]

Thus every sense consists of clusters of matter (*dravya indriya*), which have two types : physical organs themselves (*nirvṛtti indriya*), and the capacity of physical organs (*upakaraṇa indriya*) and the modes of soul which are also of two types — sentient potential (*labdhi indriya*) and sentient application (*upayoga indriya*).

The sentient potential (*labdhi indriya*) causes the physical organs (*nirvṛtti indriya*) which causes the capacity of organs (*upakaraṇa indirya*) and then sentient application (*upayoga indriya*) is caused.[6] This may be known as below.

1. Sentient potential (*labdhi indriya*)
2. Sentient potential, physical organs (*nirvṛtti indriya*)
3. Sentient potential, physical organs, capacity of organs (*upakaraṇa indriya*)
4. Sentient potential, physical organs, capacity of organs and sentient application (*upayoga indriya*).

It means that there can be no sense in the absence of Sentient Potential.

Names of Senses

Senses are known as the different parts of the body in the following way:[7]

1. Sense of touch (*sparśendriya*) — Skin.
2. Sense of taste (*rasendriya*) — Tongue.

---

5. That Which Is (*Tattvarthā-Sūtra*), tr. Nalahamal Tatia, p. 43.
6. *Tattvārtha-Sūtra*, tr. Sukhalal Sanghavi, p. 57.
7. Ibid.

3. Sense of smell (*ghrāṇendriya*) — Nose.
4. Sense of sight (*cakṣurindriya*) — Eye.
5. Sense of hearing (*śrotrendriya*) — Ear.

Every sense is the combination of *nirvṛitti, upakaraṇa, labdhi* and *upayoga.* But the question arises that if *upayoga* is the result attained through senses, how can it be addressed as sense? The answer is: though *upayoga* is the result or work of *nirvṛtti, upakaraṇa* and *labdhi,* it may be treated as sense because result or work is always included in its cause.

Objects of Senses[8]

Touch is the object of the sense of touch.
Taste is the object of the sense of taste.
Smell is the object of the sense of smell.
Sight is the object of the sense of sight.
Sound is the object of the sense of hearing.

Mind

Mind is known as non-sense (*anindriya* or non-*indriya)* because it is too subtle. It is also addressed as internal organ. The articulate knowledge (*śruta jñāna*) is considered as its object.[9]

Beings

The following table presents the names of beings and their capability of having different senses.[10]

---

8. *sparśa rasāgandha varṇaśabdasteṣa marthaḥ* 121 ibid.
9. *śrutamanindriyasya* 221 ibid.
10. That Which Is (*Tattvārtha-Sūtra*), tr. Nalahamal Tatia, pp. 45-46.

Number of Senses	*Beings*
One Sense (Touch)	Earth, Water, Fire, Air and Plants.
Two Senses (Touch and Taste)	Worms, Leeches, Snails, etc.
Three Senses (Touch, Taste and Smell)	Ants, Fleas, Plant Lice, Centipedes, Insects, etc.
Four Senses (Touch, Taste, Smell and and Sight)	Flies, Mosquitoes, Butterflies, Moths, Scorpions, etc.
Five Senses (Touch, Taste, Smell Sight and Hearing)	Animals,Fish, Birds, Quadrupeds, Humans, etc.

Senses and Knowledge

According to the Jaina way of thinking, there are five varieties of knowledge.[11]

1. Empirical knowledge (*mati-jñāna*)
2. Articulate knowledge (*śruta-jñāna*)
3. Clairvoyance (*avadhi-jñāna*)
4. Mind-reading (*manaḥ paryāya-jñāna*)
5. Omniscience (*kevala-jñāna*)

The empirical knowledge is achieved through senses and mind. The articulate knowledge is gained through the sacred scriptures. The remaining three are obtained through soul. These are independent of senses.

Generally, knowldege is divided into two categories: (1) Direct knowledge (*pratyakṣa-jñāna*) and (2) Indirect knowledge (*Parokṣa-jñāna*). The direct knowledge is attained through senses and mind, i.e. touch, taste, smell, sight, hearing and mind. But in Jainism, the knowledge gained through senses and mind has been considered as the indirect knowledge

11. *matiśrutavadhimānaḥparyāyakevalāni jñānam* 91, *Tattvārtha-Sūtra*, tr. Sukhlal Sanghavi, p. 91.

(*parokṣa-jñāna*). The knowledge achieved through soul is the direct knowledge (*pratyakṣa-jñāna*). Later on Akalaṅka, a great Jaina logician divided knowledge into three classes:

(i) *Pāramārthika pratyakṣa,* the real perception or the direct knowledge which is obtained through soul.

(ii) *Sāmavyāvahārika pratyakṣa,* which is gained through senses and mind, and that which has been accepted as perception in the practical life. It means that *sāmavyāvahārika pratyakṣa* is that which has been accepted as perception in the practice of common life; though in real sense it is not a true perception.

(iii) *Parokṣa-jñāna,* i.e. indirect knowledge which consists of inference, memory, etc.

Senses and Non-violence

The term non-violence is the combined form of two words *non* and *violence,* i.e. negation of violence or absence of violence. But the question arises: What is violence? Umāsvāti has defined violence (*hiṁsā*) in the following *sūtra*: *pramattayogāt prāṇavyāropaṇam hiṁsā.*[12]

The violence occurs when the vitality of a *jīvā* is destroyed due to envy or enmity. "In the *Sarvārthasiddhi,* the element of vitality is added to explain the nature of all beings, irrespective of how many senses they have. There are ten vitalities"[13] : (1) Sense of touch, (2) Body, (3) Respiration, (4) Lifespan, (5) Sense of taste, (6) Faculty of speech, (7) Sense of smell, (8) Sense of sight, (9) Sense of hearing, and (10) Rationality. From the table given below one can know the different beings having different vitalities according to the sense they have.

---

12. *Tattvārtha-Sūtra,* Chapter 7.
13. N.M. Tatia, pp. 42-43.

Beings	*Vitalities*
One sensed being	From one to the 4th vitality
Two sensed being	From one to the 6th vitality
Three sensed being	From one to the 7th vitality
Four sensed being	From one to the 8th vitality
Five sensed non-rational being	From one to the 9th vitality
Five sensed rational being	From one to the 10th vitality

Thus, senses have been discussed by the Jaina thinkers in their own way.

6

Senses and Human Understanding

B.D. Tripathi

LET me begin this paper with a quote from Immanuel Kant's book, *Critique of Pure Reason.*

> Though all our knowledge begins with experience, it does not follow that it arises from experience.[1]

Kant further poses a question,

> Whether there is any knowledge that is thus independent of experience and even of all impressions of the senses? Such a knowledge is entitled a priori and distinguished from the empirical, which has its sources a posteriori, that is, in experience.[2]

Now, start from the very beginning. There are Five senses, namely, eye, nose, ear, tongue and skin. These senses convey knowledge of the outer world to the human mind in the form of vision, olfaction, audition, gustation and touch respectively. Let it be mentioned here that out of the five senses, four are dual-sensory and the remaining one is uni-sensory. In addition to their own specific sensations, eyes, nose, ears and tongue also convey touch-sensation to the mind. Skin conveys only one sensation to the mind that is, touch. The five senses are

1. Immanuel Kant, *Critique of Pure Reason,* London: Macmillan, 1929, p. 41.
2. Ibid., pp. 42-43.

further classified into two categories, namely, contact and distance. Contact senses convey impressions from the stimuli to the mind through contact. Tongue and skin fall in the contact category of senses. They convey gustation and touch messages respectively to the mind only after the physical contact with the stimuli. Eye, ear and nose are distance senses. They catch impressions from their respective stimuli, both from afar, as well as from close ranges.

Senses are the media of perception; they cannot perceive themselves. Delinked from the mind, they lose all capacity to perceive. It is generally believed that senses and stimuli play active and passive roles respectively in the perceptual process. Such a belief, however, is belied quite often. Two bulls fighting with each other, forcibly catch the attention of people around. Further, sense's perceptual jurisdiction is confined to the outer world; they cannot look within. A hymn in *Kaṭhopaniṣad* clearly states that senses are so constituted as to perceive the outer world only; they cannot orient their focus in the inner world of man.[3]

Let us distinguish perception from other neighbouring words such as sensation, sensitization and observation. Sensation is a pre-stage of perception. Sensation arises when the senses come in the tangential touch with the stimuli. Sensation is believed to be a psychological myth. Sensitization is a process wherein senses derive impression from the *stimuli.* Observation is planned and purposive perception.

Limitation of Senses

Īśvara Kr̥ṣṇa, author of *Sāṁkhya-Kārikā* enumerates certain limitations of visual perception.[4] According to him, under

3 *parāñci khāni vyatr̥ṇat svayambhū stasmāt parāṅpaśyati nāntarātman.*
kaścid dhīraḥ pratyagātmānamaikṣad āvr̥ttacakṣuramr̥tatvamicchan.
— *Kaṭhopaniṣad* 2.1-1.

4. *atid]ūrāt sāmīpyādindriyaghātānmano 'navasthāt* ।
saukṣmyādavadhānādabhibhavāt samānāvihāracca ॥
— *Sāṁkhya-Kārika* 7

certain circumstances, eyes convey false knowledge of the stimuli to the mind. Visual limitations arise under the following five conditions.

(A) EXTREMELY CLOSE CONTIGUITY WITH THE STIMULI

A dust particle falls in the eyeball. The particle is so close to the eye, yet the eye fails to perceive it. Further, eyes fail to perceive their own eyebrows because of the same reason. In fact, the visual focus has a starting as well as termination-point. Stimuli at the pre-starting point fall without the range of visual perception. The termination-point of focus is extended in the case of radiant objects, such as the sun, the moon and the stars. In the case of non-radiant objects, the termination-point occurs much earlier. It is because of this tendency of visual termination that the sky falsely appears as a canopy. The canopy-view of sky is nothing but an illusion that arises due to the termination-tendency of the visual perception. Let it be mentioned here that sensory perception is confined only to such stimuli which physically exist. Sky lacks this qualification; it is devoid of all physical attributes. In Sanskrit language, the equivalent of sky is *śūnya*. Void or *śūnya* lies beyond the periphery of visual perception. Our knowledge of sky, therefore, is not perceptual; it is inferential. Like sky (space), the entity of time also lies beyond the periphery of visual perception. Yet it is believed to be a piece of empirical reality. In fact, the origin-point of the time-concept is traceable to the sequence of astral events such as sun-rise, a sun-set, hide-and seek-play of day and night, cycle of seasons and so on.

(B) INATTENTION

In the state of inattention, divided attention, sleep and other such mental conditions, eyes along with other senses cease to perceive any stimuli. In the state of inattention, linkage of mind with the senses is suspended.

(C) INFINITESIMALITY OF THE STIMULI

In the event of the infinitesimality of the stimuli, there is no perception of the items concerned. We fail to perceive small germs, atom particles. We fail to form auditory sensation of sound, if it dips below a minimum volume.

(D) STIMULI UNDER COVER

Our eyes fail to perceive such stimuli, which are not exposed to them directly. We do not perceive our lungs, heart and other inner parts of body as they are covered by the skin and flesh.

(E) IDENTICAL STRUCTURE OF UNITS

Our eyes fail to distinguish identical units from one another. We fail to distinguish one ant from the other, one fly from another, one bee from another, one wasp from another and so on.

Further, according to Īśvara Kṛṣṇa, our eyes convey false knowledge of the stimuli to the mind under the following three conditions:

First, Jaundiced eye conveys false message to the mind in respect of the stimuli's colour. Second, stimuli lying far away from us, do not appear as big as actually they are. The sun, the moon, the stars, appear so small and tiny, which is evidently a false knowledge. Third, under dazzling light of the sun, we fail to perceive the stars. In other words, glory of stars is lost in the radiant light of the sun. Non-perception of the stars in the daytime is a piece of false knowledge which our eyes convey to the mind.

The story of non-perception, wrong perception and perceptual limitation does not end over here. There are many more instances wherein our senses fail to perceive the stimuli as actually they are. Our senses openly mislead us. There are cases of illusion (rope appearing as snake). Perception of movement outside the running train is another example of perceptual illusion. Hallucination (perception of apparition and other non-beings, non-perception of stimuli due to darkness are the common experiences of our life. Further, our senses convey false knowledge in respect of stimuli of enormously large size. Due to the largeness of the earth, it appears as flat, though it is global in constitution. The list of visual limitations and false perception in fact, is quite long and serpentine.

A poet composed a rhyme, which reads as below:

Twinkle twinkle little star. How I wonder what you are.
Up above the world so high. Like a diamond in the sky.
When the burning sun is set. When the grass with dew is wet.
Then you show your little so light. Twinkle twinkle all the night.

In this rhyme, three pieces of false knowledge have been conveyed to the reader (tiny tots). First, the star is diamond-sized. Second, the sun sets, and the third, it twinkles in the night only and not in the daytime.

Limitations of human senses are overcome by technologies developed by man. Distant sounds are brought within the reach of man's auditory perception through radio, telephone and mobile phones. Distant images are brought within the reach of man's visual perception through TV. Man perceives inner parts of the body through X-ray. Man extends his perceptual capacity through such instruments as telescope, microscope and many such others.

I view the problem of perceptual limitation and human senses coveying false knowledge to the mind in a different way. In my view, the knowledge, which senses supply in respect of stimuli, is *primary*. A parallel may be drawn between primary knowledge and raw gold extracted from the gold mine. At the later stage, man processes his primary knowledge and raises it to the secondary stage. At the secondary stage, the sense data are *checked* and *balanced.* Through the process of checking and balancing, man approximates his knowledge to the real state of the stimuli.

Through his sustained experience, man tries to explicate the nature of perception and *devises* ways and means to pick up true pieces of knowledge from the heap of mixed data supplied to him by the senses.

Our senses supply us primary or raw data. As the senses are the part of the nature, they are constrained to abide by the laws of nature. Nature has framed the law of *diminishing size* in respect of long-distance perception. Our senses cannot outstrip such laws. According to the law of diminishing size, the image of the stimuli grows smaller and smaller with the rise of distance between the two sides of perception. After man comes to know this law, he does not interpret his perceptual data literally. He changes his mode of interpretation in the light of the law of diminishing image.

If man does not perceive stars in the daytime, he does not rely on the testimony of the daytime sense data. For true knowledge, he moves to the nocturnal data in respect of the stars. Man now knows why things outside the moving train appear as moving. The man at the present stage of awareness has freed himself from the wrong pieces of knowledge lying buried in the heap of primary data. Jaundiced man does not rely on the sense data in respect of the colour of the stimuli supplied by his diseased eyes. There are others to tell him the true colour of the stimuli.

In addition to the natural laws by which our senses abide, there are certain tendencies of perception. These tendencies have been identified by some psychologists. According to Krech and Crutchfield,[5] visual perception is determined by two sets of factors, *structural* and *functional*. Structural factors derive from the structure of the stimuli. Following are the major structural factors which determine the nature of perception:

(a) ***Contiguity*** — Two items immediately contiguous to each other are seen as part of the common stimuli.

(b) ***Closure*** — Two separate units if united, looks as one unit.

(c) ***Figure and Ground*** — Figure is perceived and ground is overlooked.

(d) ***Whole and Part*** — Whole is perceived as a single unit and the parts are lost in the whole unit. We perceive the tree but hardly perceive its leaves individually.

(e) ***Similarity of Items*** — Similar items of the stimuli are perceived as parts of a single structure. This is called similarity principle of perception. Murphy[6] has given a detailed and illustrated description of the structural factors of perception.

Functional factors derive from man's needs, moods, personal idiosyncrasies, past experiences, memory, mental set and several such personality dispositions of the persons concerned. Functional factors go to make perception selective. People ignore certain items of the stimuli inadvertently and selectively perceive such items which suit to their needs. A hungry man may perceive non-eatable items as eatable ones.

Now, how man picks up pieces of true knowledge from the mixed heap of sense data? Does he rely for this on anything other than the senses? This is a very crucial question.

---

5. David Krech and Richard S. Crutchdfield, *Theory and Problems of Social Psychology;* New Delhi: McGraw Hill, 1948, pp. 76-109.

6. Gardener Murphy, *An Introduction to Psychology,* New Delhi: Oxford and IBH Publishing Company, 1964, pp. 156-80.

On this issue, views furiously differ. Philosophers and epistemologists are divided into two schools on this point, *empiricism* and *rationalism*. Propositions posited by one school are hotly refuted by the other. Empiricists like Locke talks of *Tabula rasa* (Blank sheet of paper) analogy. On the other hand, rationalists like Leibniz talk of *windowless monads*. Whereas empiricist economy is based on the policy of endless import, rationalist economy follows the policy of total self-sufficiency. The two extremes were joined by Kant. He came out with the concept of a priori and a posteriori. Kant was half empiricist and half rationalist in his approach. According to him, truth does not lie in either of the two schools; rather it consits in the synthesis of a priorism with a posteriorism.

Analogically speaking, Lockian man is settled on the moon. For his sustenance and subsistence on the lunar surface, he imports his necessary items from the earth as nothing grows on the surface of the moon. Like lunar surface, man's mind does not produce anything internally; it simply imports items from without through servants (senses) and cooks the material thus collected. Entire property of mind is collected from the outside sources. If this be the position of Locke, he is certainly indefensible. But Locke is not so categorical on this point. According to him, man's mind is not equipped with *innate ideas*, but it certainly is equipped with *innate faculty*.

Quite unlike the Lockian man, Leibnizian man is lodged in a cell, where everything is provided from the very beginning once and for all. Here, there is a rule of *pre-established harmony*. Mind need not move out of the cell for anything. Leibnizian man's cell is closed from all the sides. The external world is strictly prohibited from entering into the monadic cell.

The Mind

As I visualize the situation, the real man is neither only senses nor only mind; he is senses plus mind. At the time of birth, the human baby is equipped with primary mind. At the initial stage, such a mind makes reflexive movements; it mechanically sustains the body; makes instinctive gestures as assisted by the primary sensory system. The senses carry the message from the outer world, which the primary mind stores, processes and synthesizes. Primary mind remains engaged in dual function, namely oozing consciousness and storing the images from the outside world conveyed by the senses. With the expanding volume of consciousness, primary mind is metamorphosed into secondary mind. Primary mind is the baby counterpart of the adult or secondary mind. In the reservoir of consciousness, sense impressions brought from the outside are shaped and fashioned. Consciousness and sense-impressions may be likened to egg and spermatozoan, respectively. The spermatozoan fertilizes the egg. The fertilized egg is nothing but *idea.* So, consciousnes is the mother and sense-impression is the father of *idea.* Both sense-impression and consciousness precede idea. In case, consciousness precedes idea, how can idea be called innate? No idea is possible without consciousness and sense-impression. Mind encompasses consciousness, idea and many other items, which it generates in course of its existence. Consciousness may also be called psychological-field, which is differentiated into several sub-systems such as cognition, affection and conation.

Primary mind is managed by the primary ego, which also goes with the name of *id.* With the growing volume of consciousness and furtherance of shade-differentiation, the *id* is metamorphosed into secondary or real ego. After coming into being, the real ego manages the volume of consciousness and directs it towards the intended targets. Primary and secondary egos may be likened to the protem or ad hoc and elected Speaker of the Parliament respectively.

Shades of Consciousness

Consciousness possesses several shades. Almost all the shades of consciousness moves under the instruction of the ego. Following are the major shades of consciousness.

(a) ***Attention*** – Attention is the flow of consciousness to a particular target. Attention takes several shapes in respect to the following conditions. *Singularity and multiplicity* of target: In the event of singular target, attention is highly pointed and intense. Multiplicity of targets makes attention fragmented, less intense and less effective with respect to each target.

(b) ***Imagination*** — It is wayward flow of consciousness towards certain distant ends. Imagination remains always tied to the string of reality like kite. Kite flies high in the sky but it does not lose touch with the ground reality.

(c) ***Inference*** — Inference is judgement reached on the basis of major and minor premises. Major premise is believed to be a piece of self-evident knowledge.

(d) ***Reasoning*** — Reasoning refers to the investment of consciousness for tentative judgement on certain issues.

(e) ***Speculation*** — Speculation is reality-controlled flow of consciousness in respect of certain issues.

(f) ***Fantasy*** — Fantasy is flight of consciousness beyond all constraints and regulations in the pursuit of certain ethereal objectives. Such a flight, however, remains under the ego.

(g) ***Dream*** — Dream is a shade of consciousness whereupon ego exercises no control whatsoever.

In this short paper, I have sought to portray the structure of human understanding and the role of senses thereinto.

7

Human Senses and their Purpose

K.N. Sahay

Human Senses

THE Five human senses, which constitute a part of Nature, have special bodily faculties by which sensations are roused — the ability to perceive the properties of things. It is a physical world through which the human organs function, building up the chemistry of life. The senses work on different parts of the body — skin, tongue, nose, eyes and ears. Sense of touch is connected with skin (*sparśendriya*); taste with tongue (*rasendriya*); smell with nose (*ghrāṇendriya*), sight with eyes (*cakṣurindriya*); and hearing with ear (*śrotrendriya*).

These senses have "Five organs of action," i.e. the mouth, hands, legs, the organ of excretion and the genital organ. Such organs are just "neutral." It constitutes means to an end. It may be used for a "bad purpose," or "good purpose." However, they do not work automatically unless there are still another four senses — four "inner organs" like the mind (*mana*), intellect (*buddhi*), memory (*citta*) and the ego (*ahaṁkāra*). Thus, in all there are nine sense-organs of the human body; the first Five are *external*, and the other four, *internal*. These modal points have long-range implications and many lead to multiplying unending things on the Earth.

Of the four inner organs, mind is the most important and powerful. As said, it receives the rays of consciousness (awareness of something opposed to becoming inert) of the soul and then activates and controls the actions of all the external organs.

> Though it is not consciousness, it moves very fast from the soul down to the external organs. . . . In fact, the mind is the "monster" which dissipates the force of consciousness through the nine outlets in the body — Sinha, 1948: 53–54.

Virtually, the nine sense-organs are considered to be the "nine gates" (*kivāṛa* as the mystic call it). The four sense-organs particularly the mind, allows the force of consciousness to go down through the senses downward, and outwardly (ibid.).

It is believed that when a man dies — the *annamaya koṣa* (food-based sheath) is terminated: Under certain circumstances the remaining four sheaths (Cosmic, Bauddhic, Astral, and Etheral bodies) may continue in the form of a "ghost," "spirit" or "ancestral-spirit." During the course of life if the person is not contented or satisfied — anger, hatred, failures, sudden death, serious expectations which couldn't fructify or the like which were uppermost in his mind — after death the "earth bound soul" haunts the family through dream or apparitions unless it is properly appeased. Human senses and the desires are so strong that even after death, feelings still continue under certain circumstances.

Besides these cases, in the higher perspective "birth-death life cycle" of the Hindu philosophy also justifies it. Rebirth works as a part of *prārabdha* (destiny) when a person reaps the harvest of his/her life — good or bad. All such activities basically constitute a part of the activities bearing with five sensory organs and the four supermost inner organs and the follow-up on reincarnation level.

Daivī Sampadā and Āsurī Sampadā

In this background, Lord Kṛṣṇa in *Śrīmad Bhagavad-Gītā* in Chapter 16:1-18, talks of men having two different types of properties (temperaments): divine (*daivī sampadā*) and demoniac (*āsūrī sampadā*). The divine property has been recognized as conducive to "liberation" and constitutes the spiritual dimension of man, while the demoniac property is conducive to "bondage" and that runs counter to the former. In this context, we would like to elaborate the *daivī sampadā* and *āsurī sampadā* which are given below:

The first three verses of chapter sixteen of *Bhagavad-Gītā* tell us about the *daivī sampadā* possessed by men of *sāttvika* disposition (Goyandka, 1978, 669-675). The first verse is —

> अभयं सत्त्वसंशुद्धिर्ज्ञानयोगव्यवस्थितिः ।
> दानं दमश्च यज्ञश्च स्वाध्यायस्तप आर्जवम् ॥ १ ॥
>
> *abhayaṁ sattva-saṁśuddhir jñāna yoga vyavasthitiḥ* ।
> *dānaṁ damaś ca yajñaś ca svādhyāyas tapa ārjavam* ॥ 1 ॥
>
> It constitutes absolute fearlessness, perfect purity of mind, constant fixity in the *yoga* of meditation for the sake of self-realization, and even so charity in its *sāttvika* form, control of the senses, worship of God and other deities as well as of one's elders and other sacred duties, study and teaching of the Vedas and other sacred books as well as the chanting of god's names and praises, suffering hardships for the discharge of one's sacred obligations and straightness of mind as well as of the body and senses.

The second verse is —

> अहिंसा सत्यमक्रोधस्त्यागः शान्तिरपैशुनम् ।
> दया भूतेष्वलोलुप्त्वं मार्दवं ह्रीरचापलम् ॥ २ ॥
>
> *ahiṁsā satyam akrodhas tyāgaḥ śāntir apaiśunam* ।
> *dayā bhūteṣv aloluptvaṁ mārdavaṁ hrīr acāpalam* ॥ 2 ॥
>
> It relates to non-violence in thought, words and deed, truthfulness and geniality of speech, absence of anger even on provocation, disclaiming doership in respect of actions, quietude or composure of mind, abstaining from malicious gossip, compassion towards all creatures, absence of attachment to the objects of senses even during their contact

> with the senses, mildness, a sense of shame in transgressing against the scriptures or usage and abstaining from frivolous pursuits.

The third verse is —

> तेजः क्षमा धृतिः शौचमद्रोहो नातिमानिता ।
> भवन्ति संपदं दैवीमभिजातस्य भारत ॥ ३॥
>
> *tejaḥ kṣamā dhṛatiḥ śaucam adroho nātimānitā* ।
> *bhavanti saṁpadaṁ daivīm abhijātasya bhārata* ॥ 3 ॥
>
> It has bearing with sublimity, forbearance, fortitude, external purity, bearing enmity to none and absence of self-esteem — these are the marks of him, who is born with the divine gift, Arjuna.

The *āsurī sampadā* or the demoniac property of man as elaborated in *Śrīmad Bhagavad-Gītā* (Chapter 16) is given as follows:

> दम्भो दर्पोऽभिमानश्च क्रोधः पारुष्यमेव च ।
> अज्ञानं चाभिजातस्य पार्थ सम्पदमासुरीम् ॥ ४॥
>
> *dambho darpo 'bhimānaś ca krodhaḥ pāruṣyam eva ca* ।
> *ajñānaṁ cābhijātasya pārtha sampadam āsurīm* ॥ 4 ॥

This verse addressed to Pārtha (Arjuna), says that hypocrisy, arrogance and pride, and anger, sternness and ignorance too — are the marks of him, who is born with demoniac properties. Such men of demoniac disposition "neither believe in the scriptures nor possess faith, and who, therefore, lead a sinful life acting on the impulse of lust, anger and greed . . ." (ibid. p. 692).

These negative attributes are further elaborated in several other verses that follow up to verse 18 in Chapter 16 and verses 1-5 in Chapter 17 of *Bhagavad-Gītā* (ibid., p. 674).

Turbulence of Senses

Senses generally lead to negative forces which is rather "convenient," like sensuousness, vanity, arrogance, anger, cruelty, hatred, jealousy and the like, and one has to culture it throughout under religious and spiritual guidance.

If you refer to cultural evolution, there was savagery, barbarism and civilization. In early society, hunters used to live in hordes. "Might is right," was the norm of the day. People were crude and didn't have higher values and there were no institutions of the sort. They had minimum norm, it was full of violence and senses were the uppermost. But in course of time, when civilization came into being, new institutions and higher values got developed and society became refined.

In Indian thought there are more than one definitions of *dharma*, and one of them was of *Yājñavalkya-Smṛti* :

> अहिंसा सत्यमस्तेयं शौचमिन्द्रिय निग्रह।
> दानं दमोदया क्षान्तिः सर्वेषां धर्मसाधनम्॥
>
> *ahiṁsā satyamasteyaṁ śaucamindriya nigrahaḥ* ।
> *dānaṁ damodayā kṣāntiḥ serveṣāṁ dharmasādhanam* ॥
>
> It tells that non-violence, truth, non-stealing, purity, control of sense-organs, charity, non-attachment, kindness and non-anger — are all the means that lead to *dharma.*

People tell that negative forces of senses go down just as water naturally flows to the lower surface. One has to control it. The alternative ideal model is of smoke, which moves always above the surface, and it is highly inspiring.

Chapter 2 of *Bhagavad-Gītā* refers to a number of *śloka*s connected with the senses, which are turbulent by nature and need to be controlled and stabilized that lead to the celestial dimension of life. At the moment, only three of them are given as follows:

> यततो ह्यपि कौन्तेय पुरुषस्य विपश्चितः।
> इन्द्रियाणि प्रमाथीनि हरन्ति प्रसभं मनः॥६०॥
>
> *yatato hy api kaunteya puruṣasya vipaścitaḥ* ।
> *indriyāṇi pramāthīni haranti prasabhaṁ manaḥ* ॥ ६० ॥

It tells that turbulent by nature, the senses even of a wise man, who is practising self-control, forcibly carry away his mind, Arjuna.

The second *śloka* tells —

दुःखेष्वनुद्विग्नमनाः सुखेषु विगतस्पृहः ।
वीतरागभयक्रोधः स्थितधीर्मुनिरुच्यते ॥५६ ॥

duḥkheṣv anudvigna-manāḥ sukheṣu vigata-spṛhaḥ ।
vīta rāga bhaya-krodhaḥ sthita-dhīr munir ucyate ॥ 56 ॥

It tells that the sage whose mind remains unperturbed amid sorrows, whose thirst for pleasure has altogether disappeared, and who is free from passion, fear and anger, is called stable of mind.

The third *śloka* tells —

यदा संहरते चायं कूर्मोऽङ्गानीव सर्वशः ।
इन्द्रियाणीन्द्रियार्थेभ्यस्तस्य प्रज्ञा प्रतिष्ठिता ॥५८ ॥

yadā saṁharate cāyaṁ kūrmo 'ṅgānīva sarvaśaḥ ।
indriyāṇīndriyārthebhyas tasya prajñā pratiṣṭhitā ॥ ५८ ॥

It tells, when like a tortoise, which draws in its limbs from all directions, he withdraws his senses from the sense objects, his mind is considered as stable.

Human Senses in Divergent Societies

Different parts and religious groups of the world have large body of similar ideas connected with human senses that lead to serious implications with varying formulations in the society. It is suggested that restrictions and be prayed as well which may lead to improvements and betterments in the society, on mundane as well as spiritual level.

Christianity pronounces that a man is made of "flesh," at the same time, it has a "spirit" and they are different (John, 3: 6). The term spirit is frequently used in the Bible to describe the character of the man who has "entered the kingdom of God" and has the "Holy spirit as the vital determining principle of his life."

In many societies, Hindus, Muslims and Christians purify themselves doing worship apart from abstention from food and drink, making charity, pilgrimage and fasting — briefly or prolonged. In this context, specifically we may refer to Muslim and Christian societies. During the month of *Ramẓān*, Muslims perform *roẓa*, and the Christians, Lent for about forty days.

The Muslims while practising *namāẓ*, the Fifth *kalamā* tells that "the Creator *Allāh* pardons all sins of the devotees — who do it mistakenly, hidingly or openly repenting the sins. *Allāh* knows everything about it and forgives their concealed sins. The original text and Hindi version (Aksi, N.D. 5) are given below:

أَسْتَغْفِرُ اللّٰهَ رَبِّىْ مِنْ كُلِّ ذَنْبٍ اَذْنَبْتُهٗ
عَمَدًا اَوْ خَطَاً سِرًّا اَوْ عَلَانِيَةً وَّاَتُوْبُ اِلَيْهِ مِنَ
الذَّنْبِ الَّذِىْٓ اَعْلَمُ وَمِنَ الذَّنْبِ الَّذِىْ لَآ
اَعْلَمُ اِنَّكَ اَنْتَ عَلَّامُ الْغُيُوْبِ وَسَتَّارُ
الْعُيُوْبِ وَغَفَّارُ الذُّنُوْبِ وَلَا حَوْلَ وَلَا قُوَّةَ
اِلَّا بِاللّٰهِ الْعَلِىِّ الْعَظِيْمِ ط

तर्जुमा — मैं अपने पालनहार अल्लाह से अपने तमाम गुनाहों (पापो) की माफी मांगता हूँ, जो मैंने जानबूझकर किये या भूलकर किये, छिपकर किये या खुल्लमखुल्ला किये, और तौबा करता हूँ मैं उस गुनाह से, जो मैं जानता हूँ और उस गुनाह से, जो मैं नहीं जानता। तू जानने वाला है ग़ैब का और छिपाने वाला है ऐबों का और बख्शने वाला है गुनाहों का।

Edward Fitzgerald who was a mathematician and astronomer wrote a famous monument — "Omar Khayyam of the *Rubaiyat*" and one of them is —

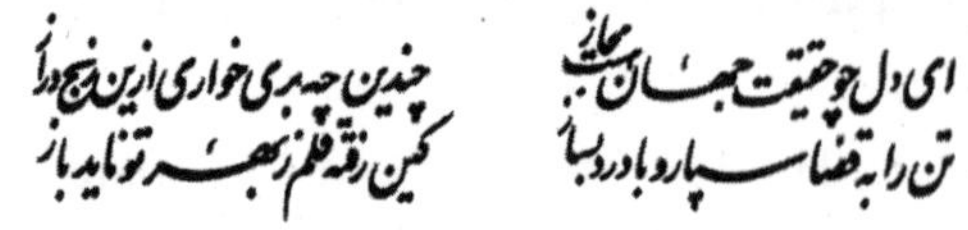

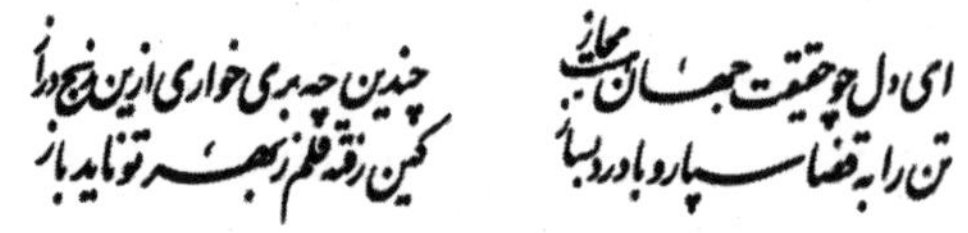

With Earth's First Clay They did the Last Man's knead,
And then of the Last Harvest sow'd the Seed:
Yea, the first Morning of Creation wrote
What the Last Dawn of *Reckoning shall read.*

Sri Sri Paramahamsa Yogananda Ji in his *Wine of the Mystic — The Rubaiyat of Omar Khayyām,* (pp. 106-07) while making the spiritual interpretation of this stanza, tells —

> Since the time of the first souls on Earth who succumbed to the desire-producing temptations of the sensory world, the kārmic effects of man's desires and actions have been the determining power in shaping each human's destiny, incarnation after incarnation. From the "last harvest's — each person's after-death state, comprising the stored, cumulative effects of all his desire and actions from his last life — the seed of unfulfilled *karma* and desire is gathered and sown in the soil of a new body in a new incarnation on Earth. Verily, from the beginning of creation, the priniciple of *karma* was written as cosmic law in the book of life. It determines the exacting judgement read to each man in the 'last dawn of reckoning' — the effects of his own free-will initiated past actions that confront him now in his present existence.

Senses and Science of Consciousness

The capacities of sense-organs, which are nature-born, are highly limited. The physical science takes the help of instruments like microscope and other scientific equipment to enhance the power of our sensory organs. But still the conscious entities remain beyond the reach of physical science and can be known only through the "science of consciousness" (*brahma-vidyā*). The knowledge thus acquired is "direct" and "flawless" (Sadafal Dev, 1978: 94-95). The power of the soul (*surati*) has infinite capacity to acquire knowledge as already referred in *Atharvaveda* (19/51/1). It tells —

I am infinitely great. I am infinitely strong in the power of my soul. The powers of eyes, ears, *prāṇa, apāna, vyāna* are all infinitely increased. I am infinite in everything.

The *śloka* follows as below:

आयुतौऽहमयुतो मे आत्मायुतं मे चक्षुरयुतं मे श्रोत्रमयुतो मे।
प्राणऽयुतो मेऽ पानोऽयुतो मे व्यानोऽयुतोऽ हं सर्वः॥

āyutau 'hamayuto me ātmāyutaṁ me cakṣurayutaṁ me śrotramayuto me ।
prāṇa 'yuto me 'pāno 'yuto me vyāno 'yuto 'haṁ sarvaḥ ॥

The sense-organs go outward and become horizontal. In case you divinize it, goes into the subtle dimension, becomes "vertical" and gets transcendental. Sense-organs become subservient and the person becomes mystic. We may refer to the famous couplet of Śrī Tulsidās of *Rāmāyaṇa* —

बिनु पग चलै सुनै बिनु काना। कर बिनु करम करै विधि नाना।
आनन रहित सकल रस भोगी। बिनु बानी वक्ता बड़ योगी॥

binu paga calai sunai binu kānā, kara binu karma karai vidhi nānā ।
ānana rahita sakala rasa bhogī, binu bānī vaktā baḍa yogī ॥

It tells that the conscious soul hears everything without ears, moves without legs, performs various actions without arms, enjoys every taste without mouth and is a great *yogī* who speaks without voice.

It may be explained in terms of *Kuṇḍalinī Yoga* in which the aspirant gets pure heart and a mind free from passions and desires. Awakening *kuṇḍalinī* benefits it and acquires different types *of siddhī* (supernatural power). It is interesting that Swami Shivananda (1971; xx-xxi) narrates that "during meditation you behold divine visions of supernatural experiences of divine smell, divine taste, divine touch, and hear divine *anāhata* sounds. . . ."

Spiritual Guidance

The disciple under the proper guidance of a spiritual-preceptor (*guru*), helps to withdraw the diffused outgoing senses and control them through *yoga,* i.e. *sādhanā* (spiritual practice) so that the force of consciousness turns inward, becomes pure consciousness and dissociates from all the physical attainments such as the mind, intellect, *prāṇa (*breath; vital essence) and the body, etc. The diffused power of consciousness need a point of convergence to "go upward," open the "tenth gate" (*daśama dvāra*) and "link up" with the *Brahman* (unqualified God), *sāra śabda* and the like.

In this context we may refer to the *Kaṭhopaniṣad* (Nikhilananda, 1949:133) which tells that there are many who do not even hear of *brahma-vidyā;* though hearing of it, many do not comprehend. Wonderful is the expounder, the rare hearer; rarer indeed is the experiencer of this knowledge taught by an able preceptor. The *śloka* is given below —

श्रवणायापि बहुभिर्यो न लभ्यः शृण्वन्तोऽपि बहवो यं न विद्युः।
आश्चर्यो वक्ता कुशलोऽस्य लब्धाश्चर्यो ज्ञाता कुशलानुशिष्टः॥
— कठोपनिषद, 1/2/7

śravaṇāyāpi bahubhir yo na labhyaḥ śṛṇvanto 'pi bahavo yaṁ na vidyuḥ ।
āścaryo vaktā kuśalo 'sya labdhā dścaryo jñātā kuśal ānuśiṣṭaḥ ॥
— *Kaṭhopaniṣad*, 1/2/7

Everybody comes across *śreya* and *preya* paths in life. Those who are intelligent and knowledgeable by analysing the pros and cons of these two paths, can prefer to chose the first one — the excellent path of true welfare *śreya,* than the second path of worldly sense pleasures, *preya*. But low intelligent people choose and adopt only the second path of *preya* from the viewpoint of fulfilling their worldly desires and lust. The *śloka* is given as follows:

> श्रेयश्च प्रेयश्च मनुष्यमेतस्तौ सम्परीत्य विविनक्ति धीरः।
> श्रेयो हि धीरोऽभि प्रेयसो वृणीते प्रेयो मन्दो योगक्षेमाद्वृणीते॥
> — कठोपनिषद्, 1/2/2
>
> *śreyaś ca preyaś ca manuṣyam etastau samparītya vivinakti dhīraḥ* ।
> *śreyo hi dhīro 'bhi preyaso vṛṇīte preyo mando yogakṣemādvṛṇīte* ॥
> — *Kaṭhopaniṣad*, 1/2/2

These refer to the higher spiritual practices and values. But before we do it, the basic pre-conditions need to be fulfilled. They are the fundamentals of moral and ethical values in higher religious groups, which constitute the stepping-stone of spiritualism that moderate and control the human senses. Some of them are kindness, charity, temperance, forgiveness, honesty, love towards all beings, self–realization, quest for truth, theism (functional), etc.

References

Aksi, n.d., *Asharfi Namaz Mutarjam* (Hindi), Delhi: Islamic Publishing Company.

Goswāmī Tulsīdās, n.d., *Rāmāyaṇa* (Hindi), Gorakhpur: Geeta Press.

Goyandka, Jaydayal, 1978, *Śrīmad Bhagavad-Gītā*, Gorakhpur: Geeta Press.

James Version, 1611, *The Holy Bible*, New York: American Society.

Nikhilananda, Swami, 1949, *Kaṭhopaniṣad*, New York: Bonaza Books.

Sadafal Dev, Maharsh, 1978, *Svarveda-Bhāṣyā* (Hindi), Part I, Gadwar, Ballia: Ādhyātmik Yantrālaya, Sadguru Sandeś Kāryālaya.

Sahay, K.N., 1998, *Spiritual Anthropology* (The Spiritual Dimension of Man), New Delhi: Commonwealth.

———, 1999, *Beyond the Thousand Petalled Lotus and the Science of Consciousness*, New Delhi: Commonwealth.

Swami Shivananda, Sri 1971, *Kuṇḍalinī Yoga*, Shivanandanagar, Rishikash: The Divine Life Society.

Sinha, K.D., 1984, "The Science of Consciousness and The Religion," in *Smarīkā* of the Vihangam Yoga Sammelan, Ranchi.

Yogananda, Sri Sri Paramahamsa, 1994, "*Wine of the Mystic — The Rubaiyat of Omar Khayyam,*" A Spiritual Interpretation, Yogananda Satsang Society of India/Self-Realization Fellowship, New Delhi: Macmillian India Limited.

8

Function of Sense-Organs in Aesthetic Perception

Kalpika Mukherjee

SARVE *svarā indrasya ātmanāḥ* — says the *Chāndogya Upaniṣad*.[1] *Ātmanāḥ*, that is the parts of the body and these parts are the *indriyas*. These sense-organs furnish bodily and mental strength. Each and every stimulus of the environment is received through the senses as also acted upon and reacted to accordingly. The Vedic *ṛṣis*, intoxicated by the beauty of nature, which they enjoyed with all their senses prayed for a long life – *paśyemāḥ śaradaḥ śatam, jīvemāḥ śaradaḥ śatam*, may we see a hundred autumns, may we live a hundred autumns. They prayed for a life prevailed by Bliss — *yatrānandāśca modāśca mudaḥ pramuda āsate* । *kāmasya yatrāptāḥ kāmās-tatra mām-amṛtaṁ kṛdhi* ॥ — where there is Bliss, Bliss and only Bliss, make me immortal by taking me to that state. It is this Bliss towards which is man's eternal journey. Directly or indirectly this journey towards the Eternal starts with the sense-organs. Hence, the *ṛṣis* of the Upaniṣads often pray for the strength of the senses, which is the starting point of every *sādhanā*. Such prayers as, *āpyāyantu mamāṅgāni vāk cakṣuḥ śrotram atha balam indriyāṇi ca sarvāni*,[2] may our *indriyas* acquire strength, may

1. *Chāndogya Upaniṣad*, Udbodhan Publication, Pt.II (*Upaniṣad Granthāvalī*) 2/22/3
2. Ibid., p. 24.

our senses of speech, sight and hearing be propitiated. For, only then we may be able to hear the good, and see what is good. We may also live a long life with our strong limbs to serve the purpose of the *Brahman*.

> *bhadraṁ karṇebhiḥ śṛṇuyāma devāḥ bhadraṁ paśyemākṣabhir-yajatrāḥ* ।
> *sthirair-aṅgais-tuṣṭuvā*ṃ*sas-tanūbhiḥ vyaśema devahitaṁ yadāyuḥ* ॥[3]

In the later parts of the Vedas itself, when the mind of the *ṛṣis* were indulged into speculation regarding the mystery of the Creation, a query flashed in their mind regarding the originator of the sense-organs. The famous Hiraṇyagarbha Sūkta of the *Ṛgveda* contains the seed of this query — *ya ātmadā baladā yasya viśva upāsate praśiṣaṁ yasya devāḥ* । *yasya chāyāmṛtaṁ yasya mṛtyuḥ kasmai devāya havisā vidhema* ॥[4] He, who gives breath, gives strength, whose commands the gods wait upon, whose shadow is immortality, whose shadow is death. The sage does not know to whom he is to offer oblation. But he knows only this much that it is Hiraṇyagarbha who was only existent initially and from whom everything has emerged. This Hiraṇyagarbha, later on *ka*, became denotative of the *Brahman*, who has been described by the Upaniṣads as beyond the senses, mind and speech and even beyond life — *śrotrasya śrotraṁ manaso mano yad* । *vāco ha vācam sa u prāṇasya prāṇāḥ* ॥[5] Now, it is the characteristic of an animal to receive the information about the environment through sense-organs. The Darwinian theory shows as to how man, the superiormost creature, came into being from the lowest creature with a single sense-organ

3. *Praśnopaniṣad* — *Śāntipāṭha*.
4. Vedic Selection, ed. Peter Peterson, Bombay Sanskrit Series, 1959, p. 46 (*ṚV* Maṇḍala–X.121.2). The same question is elaborated later on in the *Kenopaniṣad* I/1. In the Hiraṇyagarbha-Sūkta, the alphabet *ka* is very significant. In the Sanskrit alphabetical system *ka* is the first consonant. The lexiconic significance of *ka* is the beginning of the universe, manifested in water with no wave.
5. *Kenopaniṣad*, I/2.

through the process of evolution and natural elimination. Creatures other than human beings are endowed with one or more than one senses. It is the privilege of man to have possesed Five senses, that of hearing (*śravaṇa*), sight (*darśana*), smell (*ghrāṇa*), taste (*svādana*) and touch (*sparśana*). The number Five being an auspicious number, many things were restricted to this particular number such as *pañcāgni, pañcāmṛtam, pañcapallavam* and so on. Besides these Five senses, man is priviledged to have possessed a sixth sense, viz. *manas*, the mind. Caraka, the sage healer, approves the traditional ascription of Five senses in man — *iha khalu pañcendriyāṇi, pañcendriya-dravyāṇi, pañcendriyādhiṣṭānāṇi, pañcendriyārthāḥ, pañcendriya-buddhayo bhavanti.*[6] Here are the Five sense-organs, the location of the Five senses, the objects of the Five senses and the cognition through the Five senses. *Manas* is, according to him, *atīndriya* beyond these Five sense-organs, *atīndriyaṁ punarmanaḥ sattvasaṅgakam "cetaḥ" ityahityeke.*[7] (In support of his own view he mentions the views of the others.) The reason for accepting *manas* as the sixth sense has been explained by Cakrapāṇidatta, his commentator as — *yadya-pi mano 'pi sukhādi-jananam prati karaṇatvena indriyam, tathā 'pi indriya-cakṣurādyādhiṣṭhayaka-viśeṣād-atīndriym ityuktam.*[8] Even though *manas* is instrumental in the recognition of the feeling of happiness and misery, etc. still as it is the dwelling place of all the sense-organs it is hence called *atīndriya* that is beyond senses. He gives an alternative explanation as — *yadi va atīndriyam iti cakṣurādibhyo 'pi atīndriyebhyaḥ sūkṣmataram duravabodhāt*[9] or because of its being subtle by far than the eyes, etc. and because of its power of comprehending the distant things it is called the sixth sense. Though each sense is

6. *Caraka Saṁhitā,* Rashtriya Sanskrit Sansthan, N. Delhi, 2002, 8/3.
7. Ibid., 8/4.
8. Ibid., Commentary, 8/4.
9. Op. cit.

associated with a special cell or a group of cells called receptors or sense-organs and each receptor responds to a special stimulus, the stimulus in every case is relayed or carried on through the nervous system to the brain and it is the brain, the *manas,* which is the coordinator of the stimulus. The task of *manas* has been clarified by Cakrapāṇidatta as *indriyaṁ cakṣurādinām yā ceṣṭā sva-viṣaya-rupādi-jñānalakṣaṇā, tatra pratyayabhūtaṁ karaṇabhūtaṁ mana iti yojyam.*[10] That is the function of senses like the eye, etc. such as the perception of form, etc. is convinced by *manas.* Cakrapāṇi enumerates the Five senses as — *tatra cakṣuḥ śrotram ghrāṇam rasanaṁ sparśanam iti,* having for their respective *viṣaya*s or objects ether, air, fire, water and earth, respectively — *khaṁ vāyur-jyotir-āpo bhūriti.*[11]

Though the senses are located in the different parts of the body, still they have an organic bond, so to say, and they act in a coordinated way. During the contact of a *viṣaya* or an object with the sense-organs, through the co-ordination of *manas,* the consciousness is revealed and the object is revealed through the contact of consciousness. This has been described by the *Kaṭhopaniṣad* as — *tameva bhāntam-anubhāti sarvaṁ tasya bhāsā sarvam-idaṁ vibhāti,*[12] on His shining everything shines and by His splendour everything becomes resplendent.

According to the Nyāya-Vaiśeṣika systems also *manas* is the *antarendriya,* an internal organ and one of the nine *dravyas* such as — *kṣiti* (earth), *ap* (water), *tejas* (fire), *marut* (air), *vyoman* (sky), *kāla* (time), *dik* (direction), *ātmā* (soul) and *manas* (mind). Jayanta Bhaṭṭa in his *Nyāyamañjarī* determines very clearly the function and status of *manas.* He says that while the other sence-organs are *bhautika* that is material things, *manas* is not so, since it has no fixed object. For, every object is regarded as the object of *manas.* Other sense-organs, in co-ordination

10. Op. cit.

11: Ibid., 8/8-9.

12. *Kaṭhopaniṣad,* II/2/15.

with the *manas* receive the objects — *manas tu na bhautikam, na niyata-viṣayam na cāsya saguṇasyendriya-bhāva iti tacca no bhautikaṁ akāryatvād-ata eva na tadupayogī na ca niyata-viṣayam yam sarva-viṣayatvaṁ tasya sakala-bāhyendryānām adhiṣṭhānatvāt.*[13] The *Vātsāyana Bhāṣya* says that since we cannot receive two things simultaneously, the existence of *manas* is to be acknowledged — *sarvārthopalabdhau nendriyāṇi prabhavanti iti sarva-viṣayam antaḥkaranām manaḥ.*[14]

The point to be discussed in this paper is how sense-organs function during the perception of a work of art. Art reproduces the raw materials of the world, not as they are, like a reflection in the mirror — *ādarśavat*, but being touched upon with the creative genius of the artist. The stimuli received through the senses from the outer world come in art in a generalized way, as the *vibhāvas*. Thus the *kāraṇas* (causes), the *kārya* (effect) in the form of bodily expressions and the *sahakārīs* (ensuents) rouse up the dormant instinct of the connoisseur and elevate him from the mundane utilitarian world. This has been explained by Paṇḍitarāja Jagannātha, an eminent aesthetician of the seventeenth century, and by Immanuel Kant in the West.

As far as the aesthetic perception is concerned, the involvement of only two sense-organs appears at the first instant. For example, in the case of music, the main transmitter is the auditory organ, whereas, in a sculpture or a painting or in a dance it is the organ of sight that is mainly involved. In the first case the melody of music received through the ear is relayed through the nervous system to the *manas*, who is the coordinator of the series of sounds and the interpreter of the meaning to the connoisseur. In the latter case, also, the whole process occurs through the *karaṇatva* or the immediacy of the

---

13. Bhaṭṭa, Jayanta, *Nyayamañajarī*, Kashi Sanskrit Series. No. 106, II, p. 67.

14. *Vātsyāyana Bhāṣya*, ed. Phanibhusana Tarkavagisa, Kalikata: Vangiya Sahitya Mandir, 1346, Vangabda.

faculty of sight. Still there remains a question as regards the involvement of other sense-organs in particular cases, which are yet to be explained, and which had not skipped the attention of the Indian epistemologists. The problem they had to deal with in such cases has been explained by the stock example of *surabhi-candanam* — the sandalwood is fragrant, where, as soon as one perceives a piece of sandalwood, one feels that it is fragrant. Clearly, two sense-organs, that is of sight and smell are involved in such cases. But even without having the smell of the sandal-wood we comment that it is fragrant, knowing fully well that the sense of sight is not competent to perceive the fragrance. The *Siddhāntamuktāvalī* deals elaborately with such cases of perception and says — *viṣayī yasya tasyaiva vyāpāro jñānalakṣaṇā* I *evam jñānalakṣaṇā, ya-asvīkāre surabhi-candanam iti jñāne saurabhāṣya jñānam kathaṁ syāt?*[15] Here the function is to be explained by *jñānalakṣaṇā* perception or how can we without acknowledging *jñānalakṣaṇā*, explain such cases as *surabhi-candanam*? In this case the sense of sight becomes directly related to the piece of sandalwood and the rest that is the fragrance is presented through memory — *smṛti*. This *smṛti* is known as *jñānalakṣaṇā-sannikarṣa*. Such perception is a combination of *laukika* and *alaukika-pratyakṣa* at a time; it is *laukika* or ordinary in so far as the sandalwood is concerned (*candanāṁśe laukikaḥ*) and *alaukika* or extraordinary in so far as fragrance is concerned (*saurabhāṁśe tu alaukikaḥ*).

In the similar way in aesthetic perception the involvement of more than one sense-organ may also be observed. In this case the "succession of our thought is not arbitrary but governed by laws — sometimes those of association, sometimes those depending upon a purpose in our thinking," says Bertrand Russell while explaining the views of Hobbes

---

15. *Kārikāvalī*, ed. A.N. Jere, Varanasi: Krishnadas Academy, 1980, p. 279 (Siddhānta Muktāvalī).

regarding sensation.[16] For example in such cases as *padmasaurabhopetaṁ mukham,* the face contains the fragrance of a lotus. The functions of the visual organ and that of smell are involved. Here the superimposition of the fragrance of lotus on the face is coupled with a particular purpose that is to suggest the charmingness of the face. Superimposition becomes prominent in cases of *samādhi-guṇa,* a quality of poetry and art in general, which has been defined by Daṇḍin, the noted poetician of the seventh century, *anya-dharmas-tato 'nyatra lokasīmānurodhinā/samyagādhīyate yatra sa samādhiḥ smṛto yathā.*[17] In *samādhi-guṇa* attribute of one object is imposed on another and the meaning is to be comprehended through the secondary usage which is known as *lakṣaṇā* in Indian epistemology and not by *abhidhā* or direct usage. In visual art, however, such superimposition occurs through the law of association.

The Mīmāṁsakas postulate *lakṣaṇā* — a second function of word to explain such meanings where the primary meaning presented by *abhidhā* becomes incompatible and hence the purport of the sentence cannot be comprehended. *Lakṣaṇā* or the secondary function of a word resides in the primary meaning, after denoting which the power of denotation becomes exhausted. Following the Mīmāṁsakas, the aestheticians also postulate this secondary power of a word which operates after the primary meaning is presented. Such cases in art may largely come under the *samādhi-guṇa*. Daṇḍin offers the following verse as an example of *samādhi-guṇa*:

padmānyar-kāṁśu-niṣṭyūtāḥ pītvā pāvaka-viprusạḥ ।
bhūyo vamantīva mukhairud-gīrṇāruṇa-reṇubhiḥ ॥[18]

---

16. Russell, Bertrand, *History of Western Philosophy,* Unwin Series, p. 533.
17. Daṇḍin, *Kāvyādarśa*, ed. Ācāryā R.C. Misrā, Chowkhamba Vidya Bhavan, 1972, I/93.
18. Ibid., I/96.

Having drunk the particles of the rays of the sun scattered over the lotuses, they are giving out the same in the form of their red filaments. The words *pītva* (having drunk), *udgīrṇa* (vomiting), and *niṣṭyūta* (spitted), have been used in their secondary sense to denote a rare charm to the lotuses. Now here the sense of sight grasps the beauty of the lotuses whereas the function of the mouth or rather the tongue and of smell (in *udgīrṇa*) through secondary usage grasp the beauty of the full-blown lotuses.

To take another example, a famous verse from the *Abhijñānaśākuntalam* of poet Kālidāsa:

anāghrātaṁ puṣpaṁ kiśalayam-alūnaṁ kararuhair
aṇābiddhaṁ ratnaṁ madhu navam-anāsvādita rasam ।
akhaṇḍaṁ puṇyānāṁ phalam-iha tadrūpam-anagham
na jāne bhoktāraṁ kam iha samupasthāsyati vidhiḥ ॥

King Duṣyanta describes the divine and pure beauty of Śakuntalā in the verse. "She is like a flower the smell of which has not been taken as yet, like a gem which has not yet been pierced, like honey that is yet to be tasted; she is like the result of a total merit. I do not know whom the destiny has kept for enjoying her beauty." The *viṣaya*s of different sense-organs such as smell, touch, taste, etc. flash forth in the mind when one goes through the verse. The aesthetic consciousness of the connoisseur is affected through the objects by means of a series of *rūpaka* (superimposition) which underlies *lakṣaṇā*. Such realization elevates the connoisseur from the micro-cosmic level to the macro-cosmic level. The stimuli of the outer world come in a generalized way and dispel the veil of consciousness (*bhagnāvaraṇā cit*) and consciousness which is self-luminous shines forth in its own splendour. This may be compared only to the *brahmāsvāda* (*brahmāsvāda-sahodara*) which is the chief purpose of art in so far as the Indian views of art is concerned.

The above survey may prompt to make a further enquiry about the functions of the Five sense-organs. In modern psychology, the sense-organs and the mind reciprocally function through motor and sensory nerves. Cakrapāṇidatta, the healing scientist, mentioned that *ātmā* comes in contact with the external or the internal experience with the five sense-organs, and with the mind as the sixth.

A line of difference in respect to the functionary of the mind and those of the sense-organs may appear as different in the modern psychology. The external objects are perceived by the five sense-organs and apperceived by the mind to appreciate good or bad, beautiful or otherwise. Aesthetic objects are therefore perceived by the five sense-organs for manufacturing the quantity and the quality of the aesthetic objects by apperception to estimate the degree of the aesthetic value.

9

Conceptual Understanding of "Five Agents" (Senses) in Chinese

Arttatrana Nayak

THE concept of "*Wu Xing*" or "Five agents" is closely linked with the Chinese theory of *yin-yang* in explaining various universal and cosmological phenomena. Both these concepts are believed to have their origins quite early, but they came to acquire much importance only during the mid-Zhou period. Three references about this are found in the ancient Chinese classics which are worth noting below.

The first reference is found in the *Selections from the Book of History*.

The Announcement at Kan

There was a great battle at Kan. The six ministers-general of his hosts were assembled. The king (Ji, son of Yu — the founder of the Xia dynasty of twenty-first century BCE) said: "O, all ye of my six armies, I have a solemn announcement to make you.

"The lord of Hu violates and despises the Five agents [metal, wood, water, fire and earth], and he neglects and discards the three proper spheres [heaven, earth, and man]. Heaven is about to cut-off his mandate; and I reverently am executing the punishment appointed by Heaven." (Theod H. Chen, *Sources of Chinese Tradition*, pp. 97-98).

The second reference is the Great Plan of the *Book of History — Recorded in Records of Historian* by Si Maqian (145?–90 BCE?) of Western Han dynasty.

The Great Plan (*hong-fan* 洪范) is the first chapter of *Book of History* (尚书) and in the first passage there is the dialogue between the first king Wu of Zhou (founder of the Zhou dynasty in eleventh century BCE) and prince Ji, which has been recorded in the book entitled *The Records of Historian* of Si Maquian. In the beginning King Wu asked: "O, Prince of Ji! The Heaven protects and offers blessings on the people living below, and it too carries out the work of surveillance over what they are doing, I don't understand this very much, how do the rules, regulations and norms operate by themselves."

The Prince in reply said: I have heard that Gǔn (鲧), the father of Yu (禹), dammed up the inundating waters and caused disorder by doing something against the basic characteristic features of water (*shui*) which constitute one of the "five elements" (*wu xing*). The God was aroused to anger and indignation and did not give him the Great Plan with the nine categories (*hogn-fan jiu-chou* 洪范九畴), as a result the normal order of the world was disrupted and damaged. As to Gǔn (鲧), he was killed, and as Yu (禹) took over the job of Gǔn as his successor. Heaven then bestowed upon Yu the Great Plan and the nine categories and the normal order of the world was thereupon restored back (*Sources of Chinese Tradition*, p. 98; Ren Jiyu (ed.), *A Brief Outline of the History of Chinese Philosophy* pp. 48-49). This is believed to be one of the really authentic accounts of the "*Wu Xing*" or the "five elements". These traditions are mentioned as examples of the way the writer of this treatise tried to give importance to the *Wu Xing* theory — As to the actual date of the "Great Plan" or this "Great Norm," modern scholarships incline to place it within the fourth or third century BCE. (Feng Yu-lan, *A Short History of Chinese Philosophy*, ed. Derk Boddge, pp. 131-32).

The third reference is to be found in the *Treatise on Literature* (ch. 30) in the *History of the Former Han Dynnasty*. This *Treatise on Literature* is based on the *Seven Summaries* by Liu Xin where the occult arts have been discussed as six classes and the third one refers to the *Five Elements* (Feng Yulan, *A Short History of Chinese Philosophy*, p. 129). "This art (phenomena) arises from the revolutions of the Five Powers [five elements], and if it is extended to its farthest limits, there is nothing to which it will not reach." (ibid).

Wu Xing or the Five Elements

The term "*wu xing*" morphologically is a combination of two individual words in Chinese such as "*wu*" and "*xing*." In Chinese "*wu*" means "five" and "*xing*" means "activities" and thus "*wu xing*" means "five activities" which have been explained in terms of five basic objects. The objects that are referred to as "*wu xing*" in the *Great Plan and Nine Categories* are: first, water (*shui* – 水), second, fire (*huo* – 水), third, wood (*mu* – 木), fourth, metal (*jin* – 金), and fifth, earth (*tu* – 土). As per the description of their nature "water has the quality and the power to descend and to soak; fire has the basic nature of blazing and ascending upwards; wood is straight and it can be crooked; metal is malleable and Earth takes seeds and it yields crops. A summary is found in the *Great Plan and the Nine Categories* about the configuration, form and function of these "five elements" : the one (water) which soaks and descends, produces saltiness (*xianwei* – 咸味), the one (fire) which blazes, by nature and ascends upwards produces "bitterness" (*kuwei* – 苦味), third, the one (wood) which is crooked or straight produces "sourness" (*suanwei* – 酸味), fourth, the one (*metal*) which has the characteristic features of being malleable produces acridity (*xinwei* – 辛味), and fifth, the one (*Earth*) which is cultivable and yield crops produces "sweetness" (*ganwei* – 甘味).

The ancient philosophers thus used to regard the objectively existing natural matters and substances (*wuzhi* –

物质) as the real and active ones, and believed that the human taste and sensation (*weijue* – 味觉) developed as a result of the man's contact with those Five different external worldly substances. The primitive men of the Shang and Zhou period of China had started forming a materialistic world outlook through their experience of daily lives and the benefits they were getting out of their surroundings (the material worlds around themselves). This concept of "Five Elements" has helped the Chinese people of later generations to further study and develop a materialist philosophy of their own. Its usage later on, is found to have been extended to explain many other cosmological and natural phenomena and the connotations of this term, consequently, have now become vast and wider in course of time. These Five elements are, thus, considered by the Chinese philosophers to be quite dynamic and interacting forces, and they are not static.

The "*Wu Xing*" has also been interpreted as "Five Functions" concerning human behaviour. The first is personal appearance; the second is speech; the third is vision; the fourth is hearing and the fifth is the thought. Personal appearance should be decorous; speech should follow order; vision should be clear; hearing should be distinct and thought is to be profound. Decorum produces solemnity; following order regularity; clearness intelligence; distinctness, deliberations; profundity, wisdom.

Growth of Human Knowledge and the Concept of Wu Xing in Chinese

The first and the basic question is how this "idea" or "concept" developed or wherefrom man's ideas develop? From time immemorial, this has become a question of utmost importance for the philosophers and saints of different schools of thought and all of them have made serious attempts to explain this from different viewpoints and approaches.

Man's ideas have been shaped and affected by his surroundings. The immediate surroundings in which man lives always do play a decisive role in shaping human ideas and attitudes from the very beginning. Man had to struggle with the "Nature" for his very survival and survival has thus become the paramount interest of the human being and he had to wage a life and death struggle against all sorts of adversaries that he encountered in the primitive society. Since this form and type of human struggle is primarily concerned with men's search for food and shelter, this may be termed as "production struggle." This is undeniably the first and the foremost struggle of the man in the history of human civilization which may be termed as one form of collectively undertaken "social practice."

Social Practice and Knowledge

As Lenin has said, "practice is higher than (theoretical) knowledge, for it has not only the dignity of universality, but also of immediate actuality." The crucial and the most advanced form of human practice that plays a decisive role in the growth and determination of human knowledge is that of man's production struggle. The Marxist philosophy of dialectical materialism holds the view that the truth of any knowledge or theory is determined not by subjective feelings, but by objective results in social practice. Only social practice can be the criterion of truth. The standpoint of practice is the primary and basic standpoint in the dialectical materialist theory of knowledge. (V.I. Lenin, *Materialism and Empirio-criticism,* FLPH, Moscow, 1952, pp. 136–42.) "Human knowledge arises from practice and in turn serves practice. Whenever man comes across the external objects he develops certain ideas and perceptions; he sees only the phenomenal side, the separate aspects and the external relations of things. This is called the perceptual stage of cognition, namely, the stage of sense perceptions and impressions and this is the first stage of cognition. At this stage, man cannot as yet form concepts, which are deeper and draw logical conclusions.

As the quality of social practice continues to improve on the basis of acquired perceptions then a sudden change (leap) takes place in the brain in the process of cognition, and concepts are formed. Concepts are no longer the phenomena, the separate aspects and the external relations of things; they grasp the essence, the totality and the internal relations of things. Between concepts and these sense perceptions there is not only a quantitative but also a qualitative difference. Proceeding further, by means of judgement and inference one is able to draw logical conclusions. This is the second stage of cognition. Man starts working out various types of relationships among the various phenomena of the outer world on the basis of his perception and understanding at this stage. And it must be noted that "this stage of conception, judgement and inference is the most important stage in the entire process of knowing (or trying to) a thing; it is the stage of "rational knowledge." The real task of knowing is through perception, to arrive at a thought, to arrive step by step at the comprehension of internal contradictions of objective things, of their laws and of the internal relations between one process and another, that is, to arrive at "logical knowledge." (*Selected Works of Mao Zedong*, vol. 1, p. 298.)

Superstitions and Knowledge

In the history of human thinking superstitions and knowledge have continued to grow side by side. Needless to say, ideas and thoughts of contemporary man have marked much advancement in all spheres of our lives today. Man has been able to unravel the mystery of nature and the operational principles of various natural and supernatural phenomena in scientific and most logical ways and manners since the beginning of the Renaissance in the fourteenth and fifteenth century of our time. Looking at the historic growth of man's ideas at various stages of development from the viewpoint of present norms and standards of human knowledge, many ideas propounded by our ancestors about all things and phenomena of the world in which we are living and the universal phenomena which we witness today seem to be loaded with certain amount of superstitions and erroneous beliefs. Nevertheless, those superstitious ideas have also helped men in propelling forward his thinking. Without that man's capacity to think would have ceased.

Historically, if we seek to place the growth of this Chinese concept of "*Wu Xing*," this is found to be the outcome of the Shang and the Zhou society. The Shang dynasty was basically a slave society and so also the Zhou society. But the Zhou period also witnessed a transition from the slave society to feudal society. It is important to examine the socio-political-economic conditions of this period to understand the emergence of this new concept and its various interpretations given by the philosophers and sages of that time.

The Zhou dynasty overthrew the Shang dynasty in the eleventh century BCE which lasted for about 800 years. The Zhou regime was a dictatorship by the slave-owning nobility with a patriarchal clan system. Under Zhou rule there were many kingdoms, some ruled by clans with the same surname as the royal house and some ruled by clans with other surnames. It was based on a coalition of the royal clan and other noble clans, with or without the same surname as the royal family, under the supreme authority of the king. The Zhou enforcement policy benefited vassals who were related to the royal house in one way or the other and this led to the development of production in a significant manner. The bronze inscriptions provide valuable information and data about the production relationship system and other cultural matters of the Zhou society.

The growth of the productive forces accompanied by serious changes of succession during the Zhou regime is believed to have exerted much influence on the socio-political-economic thought system of this period. It is relevant to note in this context that the failure of the former Shang king to adhere to the throne and their success in wresting the power from Zhou too influenced their thinking of divination. When the Zhou tribes came to rule over the middle kingdom, they admitted that the Shang kings were the elder sons of the Lord on high, but since they had failed to live up to his expectations, the Lord on high shifted his favour from the east to the west. As the Zhou dynasty embodied the divine will, it was given supreme power over the human world. But the mandate of heaven was not permanent; it depended on whether the conduct of posterity met with the approval of heaven. Here again the ancestral god became separated from the supreme God, because the former was not the only son of the latter. It seems that the supreme god of the Shang was autocratic, while that of Zhou, though autocratic, was also rational. The Shang god belonged to the Shang alone, while the Zhou god did not, but stood above dynasties and tribes. In this respect the Zhou religion was more developed than the Shang religion, and this also reflected the political ideas of the Zhou dynasty in its early period. (Bai Shouyi, *An Outline History of China*, pp. 82-83.)

This theory of "Five Agents" assumed much importance during the Qin period in its application to history and the succession of dynasties. As each season is ruled by an agent, so it was believed, each dynasty rules by virtue of an agent which it honours by adopting the colour of the agent, in its vestments and flags, and by similar ritual observances. The first emperor of the Qin, for instance, believing that his dynasty was ruled by the virtue of the power of water, adopted black as his official colour and even changed the name of the Yellow river to "Powerful Water" (*te-shui*).

During the period of the former Han dynasty, Dong Zhonshu made great use of the cosmological theories of the *yin-yang* and five agents in formulating his system of Confucian philosophy. So closely are these concepts woven into all of his other ideas that it is impossible to separate his cosmological explanations from his political or ethical theories.

One important effect of establishing this relationship between these concepts and ideas of the *yin-yang* and the "Five Agents" with the political establishments of the time is that it greatly helped the ruling elites to generate a new conviction and faith in the minds of the common people about their legitimacy to rule over the land. Thus the theory of the dynastic cycle in explaining the growth of Chinese history too has greatly helped the later historians to study Chinese political philosophy.

10

Sensitivity of Japan

Hikotaro Furuta

JAPAN is one of the nations that has the highest sensitivity in the world. It is because of the distinguished four seasons with beautiful sceneries, food, etc. in Japan. The sensitivity of Japanese people that has grown up in such natural environment reached a remarkable level. Therefore, their senses were sharpened and brought about a flash of the sixth sense so-called "Kan" or intuition, and cultivated depth of Japanese culture.

Once Yasunari Kawabata mentioned about the beauty of Japan that can be expressed by a poetical word, "The time of the snows, of the moon, of the blossoms — then more than ever we think of our comrades," in his commemoration lecture at the Nobel Prize in Literature, 1968.

> When we see the beauty of the snow, when we see the beauty of the full moon, when we see the beauty of the cherries in bloom, when in short we brush against and are awakened by the beauty of the Four seasons, it is then that we think most of those close to us and want them to share the pleasure. The excitement of beauty calls forth strong fellow feelings, yearnings for companionship and the word "comrade" can be taken to mean "human being." The snow, the moon, the blossoms, words expressive of the seasons as

> they move one into another, include in the Japanese tradition the beauty of mountains and rivers and grasses and trees, of all the myriad manifestations of nature, of human feelings as well. — *Japan, the Beautiful, and Myself,* tr. Edward G. Seidensticker.

When we see the classical literature of Japan, it can be recognized how Japanese people could find beauty in nature and perceive it sensitively. Such sensitivity that can respond to the delicate changes of nature and appreciate beauty by using not only sight but also all the senses which had been originally cultivated by Japanese people themselves.

Moreover, natural beauty occupies an extremely important position in Buddhism such as Zen. According to the traditional Buddhism, attachment of pleasant feelings should be abandoned, but Japanese Zen aims to shine nature itself beautifully by abandoning self-consciousness, and "Satori" or enlightenment is a realization of oneness without any distinction between nature and oneself. Thus, Japanese sensitivity can be seen in Japanese culture that has been brought up with various impressions by nature.

However, these sensitivities began to decline among Japanese people in the modern technological society. It remarkably appears in the children's sensory functions. In the past, the growth of senses of children had been naturally acquired by playing with Nature, but now shows the tendency of degeneration by living in the machine civilization. The appearance shows mechanization of human senses such as no sensation of pain in the body, no impression in spite of seeing and listening to beautiful works, paralyzed taste and smell, etc.

All creatures have repeated evolution and degeneration since ancient times, and mankind came out, though no one knows their destination in future. The end may be waiting for us as inclined deformity that uses only particular organs after throwing useless senses and functions which are not adjustable in the society.

The culture which was created by human beings, who lost their sensations, has been naturally deformed, and there is no virtue such as compassion or love which has been kept in mankind. What kind of sense of value is created by mankind who only has mind like a stone that does not feel other's pain and suffering but can pursue personal facilities and comfort only?

It is not known much that Japan which is a successful country and a target for all developing countries in Asia that has fallen into the crisis of losing senses. If the end of machine civilization means the society which only creates deformed human beings, it is an extremely regrettable phenomenon in the whole history of mankind.

Recently, the people who realized the crisis of sensation started a movement of regeneration of senses in Japan. They try to escape from the environment which is enclosed by machines and to regenerate their senses by touching with nature. Because mankind was not created by machine, but nature. By the touch of nature, the organs of sensation can recover the functions they have kept in themselves originally.

Rabindranath Tagore once praised the sensitivity of Japan as "quiet sensitivity of perfection" that we should not lose it. The heart of Japanese culture can be succeeded only by the sensitivity for the realization of perfection.

11

Dual Nature of Senses
Islamic View

A.S. Inam Shastri

ALL the physical parts of the human body are equally important and play important roles to keep the man active and alive. There are Five sense-organs. They are ear, nose, eyes, lips/tongue and skin. These organs are important to hear, smell, see, taste/speak and feel. A man becomes handicapped and his life becomes a challenge if these organs are imbalanced. However, it is a matter of detailed discussion and a long time is needed for its elaboration. A number of papers are already presented highlighting the importance of sense-organs.

Here, I wish to indicate about the sensitiveness of certain parts and organs of human body as per the Holy Koran.

It is indicated in Mu-munun

"Man We did create
From a quintessence (of Clay),"

In this beautiful passage, God's creative work, as far as man is concerned, is recapitulated, in order to show man's real position in this life, and the certainty of the future: to which he was referred for his regard in other verses (10-11).

Sura Baqara (ii-30)

Behold, thy Lord said to the
angles: "I will create

> A vicegerent on Earth." They said,
> "Wilt Thou place therein on who will make
> Mischief therein and Shed blood?
> Whilst we do celebrate Thy praises
> And glorify Thy holy (name)?"
> He said: "I know what ye know not."

It would seem that the angels, though holy and pure, and endued with power from God, yet represented only one side of creation. We may imagine them without passion or emotion, of which the highest flower is love. If man was to be endued with emotions, those emotions could lead him to the highest and drag him to the lowest. The power of will or choosing would have to go with them, in order that man might steer his own bark. This power of will gave him to some extent a mastery over his own fortunes and over nature, thus bringing him nearer to the God-like nature, which has supreme mastery and will. We may suppose the angels had no independent will of their own. Their perfection in other ways reflected God's perfections but could not raise them to the dignity of vicegerency. The perfect vicegerent is he who has the power of initiative himself, but whose independent action always reflects perfectly the will of his principal. The distinction is expressed by Shakespeare (sonnet 94) in those Five lines: "They are the lords and owners of their faces. Others but stewards of their excellence." The angels in their one-sidedness saw only the mischief consequent on the misuse of the emotional nature by man; perhaps they also, being without emotions, did not understand the whole of God's nature, which gives and asks for love. In humility and true devotion to God, they remonstrate: We must not imagine the least tinge of jealousy, as they are without emotion. The mystery of love being above them, they are told that they do not know, and they acknowledge not their fault but their imperfection of knowledge. At the same time the matter is brought home to them when the actual capacities of men are shown to them.

Sura Baqara (ii-31)

"And He taught Adam the nature
Of all things; then He placed them
Before the angels, and said; "Tell Me
The nature of these if ye are right."

The literal words in Arabic throughout this passage are: "The names of things," which commentators take to mean the inner nature and qualities of things; and things here would include feeling. The whole passage is charged with mystic meaning. The particular qualities or feelings which were outside the nature of angels were put by God into the nature of man. Man was thus able to love and understand love, and thus plan and initiate, as becomes the office of vicegerent. The angels acknowledge this. These things they could only know from the outside, but they had faith, or belief in the unseen. And they knew that God saw all what others see, what others do not see, what others may even wish to conceal. Man has many qualities which are talent or which he may wish to suppress or conceal to his own detriment.

Further, as indicated in *Sura Ha-Mim* (*Sajda*) XLI-20

At length, when they reach
The (Five), their hearing,
Their sight, and their skins
Will bear witness against them,
As to (all) their deeds.

All the members of their bodies and the faculties of their mind, which they misused, will bear witness against them. Similarly, their hands and their feet bear witness against them (*Sura Yasin* XXXVI-65). The "skin" not only includes the sense of touch but also the sense of taste and sense of smell, which are specialized forms of the organ of touch.

All the sensory organs and all their intellectual and emotional counterparts advance us by their use and pull us down by their misuses. They become tell-tale witnesses against us if abused.

Sura He-Mim Sajda (XLI-21)

"They will say to their skins:
"Why bear ye witness
Against us?" They will say:
"God hath given us speech, —
(He) Who giveth speech
To every thing: He created
You for the first time,
And unto Him were ye
To return."

A new phase of their existence will now dawn on them. They used to think that if they concealed their evil deeds from the rest of the world, nothing would happen to them. But God can give "tongue to trees," and can make every fact in life, known and unknown to the world, contribute to the elucidation of truth and justice. "Speech," on behalf of their senses and faculties should of course be understood figuratively. When we succumb to evil our limbs and faculties themselves betray us.

Sura He-Mim Sajda (XLI-22)

"Ye did not seek
To hide yourselves, Last
Your hearing, your sight,
And your skins should bear
Witness against you But
Ye did think that God
Knew not many of things
That ye used to do."

The limbs and faculties will say, "You did not seek to hide your evil from us: In fact you used us for your evil, because we were in your power. Did you not know that God knew everything and that our knowledge would be evidence against you?"

It is worth to discuss the state of man, when focusing on sensory organs. The Holy Koran observes *physical, moral* and *spiritual* state of man.

1. NAFS-i-AMMARA

Nafs-i-Ammara is the source of physical state of man. This state signifies the uncontrollable spirit or the spirit proved to be evil. As per its characteristic, it inclines man towards evil, tends to lead him into iniquitous and immoral paths and stands in the way of his attainment of perfection and moral excellence. (Sura Yusuf: 54)

2. NAFS-i-LAWWAMA

It is a moral state of man when a transformation is worked in his soul from grossness to virtue, he then passes out of the physical state and becomes a moral being.

According to the Holy Koran:

> "And I call to witness the spirit
> that blames itself (on every
> dereliction of duty or on the
> slightest act of disobedience
> being conscious of having offended)
>
> — *Sura Al-Qiyamah*

At this stage the soul is anxious to attain moral excellence and revolts against disobedience which is the characteristic of the first state or the animal stage, but does not withstand its yearning for virtue, sometimes deviate from the line of duty.

3. NAFS-i-MUTMAINNAH

The soul in this stage is, in the words of the Holy Koran, the Nafs-i-Mutmainnah or the soul of rest. Thus it says:

> "O thou soul that art at rest
> (and restest fully contented
> with the Lord), return to thy Lord,
> thou being pleased with Him and
> He pleased with thee; so enter
> among My servants and enter
> into My paradise."

At this stage the soul is freed from all weaknesses and frailty and is braced with spiritual strength. It is perfectly united with God and cannot exist in separation from Him. It is further clear that it is in this life and not after death that this great transformation is worked and that it is in this world and not elsewhere that access to paradise is granted to it. The love of God is its sustenance and it drinks deep at this fountain of life and is therefore delivered from death.

As per Holy Koran, as mentioned under a number of verses regarding the sensory organs like hearing, sight, skins, limbs (hands and feet), their intellectual and emotional counterparts as well as faculties are under the control of a man like a slave. They follow the orders of their master during the life-span. But, after the death, on the Day of Judgement, God will give them tongue and the sensory organs will bear witness against the man. Then there will be no way out.

12

Christian Understanding of Five Senses

D.M. Solomon

For just as the body is one and has many members, and all the members of the body, though many, are one body. . .

— 1 *Corinthians* 12:12

THE body is deeply symbolic in human culture. The body is the proximate object of our experience; it becomes a vehicle for attaining the world in its manifold aspects and dimensions. Persons and communities express themselves to the fullest through bodily language of gestures, signs, and actions. Culturally-bound signs and symbols that are intimately linked to the body often accompany the verbally communicative language. The aspirations and anxieties of a society are played out in the human body by such activities as fasting, whipping, touching, dancing, weeping and listening to God's word. It would not be an exaggeration to say that the world-view of a culture could be mapped out by deciphering body's invisible language. Only in a body, a self is realized and the common experience tells us that body and self are one unitary element to be experienced. Man's existence then is defined by his bodily existence, which gives a philosophical certainty to his being. Man then does not merely have a body but he is body. Corporeality, though limited in space and time, allows us to express the spiritual base of our actions concretely. — *Sacramentum Mundi,* 1 1969:234

It is in this sense, the Christian theology has applied analogy of faith and being for the understanding of body as the true recipient and site of revelation. One could say that embodiment is the heart of Christian structure for "Word became flesh and dwelt among us" (John 1:14) namely, God becoming man, is the beginning of Christian theology. So also, for a Christian believer, faith in the bodily resurrection of Jesus is a prerequisite for the promised experience of transformed bodily existence in the heavenly kingdom. Any discourse, then, on Five senses of body could be explainable only in the light of historical theological deliberations on the understanding of body.

The first part of the paper throws light on the debate over the dualistic and integral nature of the body, and the second part of the paper deals with the bodily senses in the light of Christian scripture. The paper concludes by pointing out the centrality of human person in Christian thought.

1. Dialectic Between Hebrew and Greek Traditions: A Christian Reinterpretation

Christian thought, in its historical development, encountered two major traditions, namely Hebrew and Greek traditions. While the initial growth of Christian thought depended on Hebrew thought stemming from the theology of the First Testament, it increasingly found itself greatly influenced as it began to spread its wings, by the well-systematized philosophy and religious universe of the Greeks. Two types of languages and thus two very different perspectives on humanity, encountering each other would lead to a rich synthesis. Jesus was from Hebrew background and the movement he started soon was emerging as an organized religion that demanded systematization of its theology and philosophy. Early Christian thinkers moulded Christian philosophy in and through Greek philosophy especially that of Plato and Aristotle. Those parts of the Greek thought that appeared to be compatible with the

Christian teachings were innovatively absorbed by the Christian thinkers. The secular Western thinking also is powerfully stamped by the Greek culture.

Theological discourse on body invariably revolves around the unity and division between body and soul that is thought of as "psyche" in Greek thought. The problematic unity between body and soul, role of sense-organs and sensations in the knowledge and ethics are chief considerations in the discourse. Here we shall limit overselves to briefly discussing the emergence of dualistic thinking in the philosophy of Plato and Aristotle as it had enormous repercussions in Christian theology and ascetic practices.

1.1 GREEK DUALISM

Rooted in the Pythagorean teaching on soul being pre-existent, immortal, divine and imprisoned by the body and relating these the doctrine of universal and unchanging Forms, Plato expounded the qualities of the soul. For Plato, the soul is the moral and intellectual personality, which is more real than body and its senses (Armstrong ND: 40). Having immortality as its nature it has to be released through the high contemplative knowledge of the divine forms. Though it is embedded in the body, it has nothing common with the senses and their faculties; the knowledge acquired by it through senses is only to assert its primacy over the body by perceiving the eternal universal truths, and the knowledge is lower in character than the knowledge acquired by contemplation on eternal form. For Plato the part played by the body and its senses in acquiring knowledge is incidental. The soul, according to Plato, is structured into three parts: First one is reason having its abode in the head and directing the whole man; second is emotions lying in the chest and finally the appetitive desires lying in the gut. The last one drives the soul downward deviating from the designed path of perfection. The body is the grave of the soul. "Salvation consists in the soul finally again 'divesting' itself of the body when on the 'island of blessed,' it attains the vision of the eternal 'ideas,' it is forever happy" (Baumert 1996: 259).

So, it is clear that soul and body could never be unified in Plato's analysis of human nature. The body is thought of as belonging to the lower realm and unworthy of man's true nature. Such a perspective was taken up by the later influential Christian thinkers like St. Augustine to deride the true unity between soul and body. Body and its exterior senses were marked as inherently evil that could potentially lead to corruption of the soul and detrimental to fuller realization of God. Such a dualistic thinking remained almost a tenet till late medieval times and influenced the thinking till modern age.

Aristotle, on the other hand, takes the changing mutable world as revealed by our senses as the point of departure for the formulation of his theory of hylomorphism — substantial unity of form and matter. The form is that which makes a thing what it is. This form informs the matter of its own constitution. The matter is that which has the potency to become what it is by the instrumentality of form. While the former is permanent and stable, the latter possesses possibility of change and therefore impermanent. This formulation coupled with the Doctrine of Act and Potency gives us the clue to the substantial unity that he posits to body and soul. If we apply the form to soul and matter to body, the substantial and essential unity is well realized. He emphasizes the intimate union of both body and soul as an organic unity. "The soul is the actuality which realizes the potentiality of a body capable of having life; it is the formative principle which makes a living body a living body" (Armstrong: 92). However, he also conceives of prime matter without any form with infinite possibility of becoming. By positing prime matter and multiplicity of forms Aristotle appears to retain the basic dualism. He also offers no explanation "for the relationship between (immortal) spirit-soul and (mortal) body-soul and hence the primordial unity of man remains obscure." (*Sacramentum Mundi:* 233).

1.2 SEMITIC TOTALITY

The Semite thought from which Biblical traditions evolved, presents a holistic picture of human person without dualistic motives. The creation of man in the *Book of Genesis* is recounted as God forming man "of dust from the ground, and breathed into his nostrils the breath of life; and man became a living being" (Genesis 2: 7). The vital breath of life does not refer to blending of two separate elements; rather it emphasizes the "livingness" of a human person. "The material of which man is made 'flesh' as soon as he is a living being" (*The Interpreter's Dictionary* 1962: 243). This word also denotes mankind, body, self, emotions and specially man as a whole, (*The New International Dictionary of New Testament Theology* (hereafter referred as *The New International* 1 1986: 672). For Hebrews, the flesh of human being is honourable as shown by writer Paul in his letter to Romans. "I appeal to you therefore, brethren, by the mercies of God, to present your bodies as a living sacrifice, holy and acceptable to God, which is your spiritual worship" (Romans 12: 1). Historical experiences within the basic conditions of human being are the starting point for integrated perspective of human nature. This integrity is well expressed through Four anthropological categories the Bible employs to describe human persons in his/her various dimensions (Baumert: 260-64).

1. The first basic condition that characterizes human being is the deficiency in the sense of compulsion, desire, dependence on people, longing for presence and relationship. The Bible uses throat in order to portray such basic desires.

2. While ordering of these desires, human beings are made conscious of the limitations and frailties. The word "flesh" is used to indicate not only the physiological reality but also powerlessness and fragility.

3. Conditions of power, vitality and energy are characterized by the word "reach" connoting wind, air, movement and breath.

4. Finally, the most important category is the "heart" illustrated by the word "Leb" (Lebanese, nationals of Lebanon). It is the seat of as diverse characteristics, attributes and qualities as knowledge, understanding, memory, insight, thinking, conscience, intentions and drives. Perceived by the Hebrew lens, heart is the vital seat of all the moral and ethical forces and therefore, susceptible to corruption.

All these four concepts stand for the entire person and human conditions. These categories evoke much more down-to-earth perceptions of human beings than abstract considerations of Greek philosophy.

1.3 A CHRISTIAN REINTERPRETATION

However, when these two streams of thought were brought together in the milieu of priestly and institutional set-up of Christianity, an ambiguous synthesis evolved in order to systematize the messages of the new religious movement. In the process of articulation and communication of the message, Greek philosophical perceptions and insights on man, nature and God were extensively adapted to the Christian concepts and framework.

St. Augustine, the influential fifth-century theologian, takes Plato's formulation of soul, ideas and forms, and applies to the understanding of body and soul retaining the basic duality of Greek culture. Though he acknowledges that man consists of soul and body, his definition of man as "a rational soul using earthly and mortal body" betrays Platonic influence. (Coleston S.J. (1) 1962: 92). He also attributes sensation to the soul and denies that knowledge gained by senses could lead one to truth. Thomas Aquinas draws Aristotle's complex structure of Form, Matter, Act and Potency for his formulation of the union between body and soul, giving it a Christian form. Aquinas stresses the natural character of unity between body and soul. "The name man applies neither to the soul alone nor to the body alone, but to soul and body together, to the composite substance." (Ibid. (2):93). The duality that is experienced "is not to be understood as a merely ontic fact but as an ontological actualization" (*Sacramentum Mundi:* 234). The soul's subsistent and spiritual nature grants the personal immortality. In spite of his assertion that soul needs the bodily senses in order to abstract knowledge, his line of argument postulating that soul does not desire the body leads to an ambiguous position.

Indeed in the following centuries this ontological viewpoint gradually recedes to the background and the dualism gains ground. Rene Descartes exemplifies the profound dualistic thinking making the reason the sole key for the unlocking of the external world. The world then becomes vast matter to be discovered, classified and controlled by the human mind (Isherwood & Stuart 1998: 71). Such a dualistic understanding was the cause of mutilation of body in ascetic practices towards disciplining the body for overcoming its supposedly inherent sinful nature. There were prescribed guidelines for protecting the bodily senses such as keeping away from aromatic perfumes, covering of hand while blessing for the purpose of avoiding touching women, restriction in the intake of particular food that will excite passion and so on. It is in this sense the Christian religion was viewed as a world-denying one.

Though at practical level the ambiguity persists, the Christian theology admits in theory that the dangers of dualism could lead to perversion of the holistic creation by God. For liberal theologians it is the person with body and soul who is redeemed and not the soul alone. Third world liberation theologians perceive salvation in a holistic manner. God is thought of as a working God who redeems people from their sinful situation. Therefore, any situation of oppression and poverty that demeans persons, are thought of sinful from which people need to be liberated. The body too must reflect the glory of God inasmuch as the interior soul. Today the philosophical and theological explanation expounds body as the primordial activity and symbolic reality and acknowledges it as the medium of knowledge of himself, seat of both noble and subhuman qualities. It is through his body and his senses he is opened to his environment, and the exterior world becomes accessible to him. Man is invited to make body as gift to others and to community (John Paul II 1981:109). Human person "in the image and likeness of God" and in the multi-dimensional existence of society and history is recognized as more important than the isolated individualistic view of body and soul.

2. Five Senses: Doors to the Presence of God

In our discussion above we have noted that the Semitic view is more holistic. Revelation is not only received by hearing or perceiving alone but through all the senses. The Biblical scholars (*The New International* (2) 1978: 173), have interpreted the usage of word "hear" as applicable to the mental process of apprehension in conjunction with the act of hearing. Invariably this process must lead the hearer to follow the precepts of the Word of God thus listened. Therefore, the sensual organs are not mere symbols for the organs of spiritual perceptions: "In them actually takes place true hearing of God's summons" (Ibid. 517). Gospel of Mark narrates a miracle of healing a deaf and dumb person in which Jesus performs series of actions ending with a touch of tongue and ears while uttering the word "be opened" (Mark 7: 31-37). The words and actions were not only addressed for the liberation of physical ailment but to the whole person. Jesus not only heals but also awakens faith in persons guiding them to appropriate the new life he offers (*The New International* 3: 860).

Inasmuch as they are vehicles for the reception of revelation, sense-organs also could take us away from the presence of God if they are not employed in accordance with the moral precepts commanded by the Lord and community. Jesus, in Sermon on the Mount, says the following:

> You have heard that it was said, 'You shall not commit adultery.' But I say to you that everyone who looks at a woman lustfully has already committed adultery with her in his heart. If your right eye causes you to sin, pluck it out and throw it away; it is better that you lose one of your members than that your whole body be thrown into hell. And if your right hand causes you to sin, cut it off and throw it away; it is better that you lose one of your members than that your whole body go into hell.
>
> — Mathew 5: 27-30

The bodily senses, then, are never views in isolation but always in view of enhancing moral man's relationship with God, world and fellowmen. Some of the organs are, indeed, associated with moral concepts and therefore attain primacy in the hierarchy of the senses. Seeing and hearing are imbued with moral qualities and they can be used interchangeably in relation to faith (*The New International* 3: 517).

An analysis of some representative passages from the Bible for each of the senses would provide us with deeper understanding of their moral, religious and social character.

3.1 SIGHT

The first passage is from the 3rd chapter, verses 7 and 9, in the *Book of Exodus*:

> Then the LORD said, "I have **seen** the affliction of my people who are in Egypt, and have heard their cry because of their taskmasters; I know their sufferings. And now, behold, the cry of the people of Israel has come to me, and I have **seen** the oppression with which the Egyptians oppress them."

Anthropomorphic qualities are attributed to God in the act of seeing implying participation in people's suffering. This participation is not a passive one but revealing the will of God to liberate them. God, then, is conceived as a living God totally involved in the history of the people.

The second passage is from the *Gospel of Mathew* in chapter 13, verses 14 and 15, wherein Jesus mourns the lack of discerning qualities among the religious leaders of the time.

> You shall indeed hear but never understand, and you shall indeed **see** but never perceive . . . and their ears are heavy of hearing, and their **eyes they have closed**, lest they should perceive with their eyes, and hear with their ears, and understand with their heart, and turn for me to heal them.

Our social position and pride often blind us from perceiving situations that demand different perspectives from the ones we are familiar with. Here, it is the cognitive faculty of discernment the author is referring to. Our sense-organ eye, then, is meant to bring self-realization and conversion of heart by being alert to the God's revelation in the world.

The third passage is also taken from the *Gospel of Mathew* in chapter 6, verses 22 and 23:

> The eye is the lamp of the body. So, if your eye is sound, your whole body will be full of light; but if your eye is not sound, your whole body will be full of darkness. If then the light in you is darkness, how great is the darkness!

The moral quality associated with eye is ascertained in order to caution the listeners from seeing either with lustful eyes, jealously or with evil intentions. Operation of senses in union with mental process of apprehension does have moral effect on the consciousness of persons and therefore, we are advised to be prudent, moderate in the indulgent use of the senses.

3.2 HEARING

Significance of hearing in Biblical revelation is much more significant than any other sense perception as man is charged with hearing the word: God meets man in his Word. The first passage is from the *Book of Isaiah*, 2nd verse of first chapter:

> Hear, O heavens, and listen, O earth,
> for the LORD speaks:
> Sons have I raised and reared,

Here, it is God who speaks in the language of men and desires them that his word is heard. Indeed the word of God is addressed to priests and prophets in the Old Testament as "The Word of the Lord came to me saying. . . ." God is qualified as personal God in whose presence men are commissioned. The solemn word of "Hear O Israel" could be a warning not to be slackening in following the command of the Lord.

For the next passage, I have taken up the parable of sower from the *Gospel of Mark*:

> The sower sows the word. And these are the ones along the path, where the word is sown; when they hear, Satan immediately comes and takes away the word which is sown in them . . . ones sown upon rocky ground, who, when they hear the word, immediately receive it with joy; and they have no root in themselves, . . . when tribulation or persecution arises on account of the word, immediately they fall away. And others are the ones sown among thorns; they are those who hear the word, but the cares of the world, and the delight in riches, and the desire for other things, enter in and choke the word, and it proves unfruitful. But

> those that were sown upon the good soil are the ones who hear the word and accept it and bear fruit, thirtyfold and sixtyfold and a hundredfold. — Mark 4: 3-20

In this passage the word "hear" implies that one uses the sense of hearing very discerningly and interpret it in order to follow it up with diligence. In fact, Jesus appears to classify people from the way we use the sense of hearing for the purpose of making the word of God fruitful in their lives. Hearing, then, brings transformation in our consciousness evoking response that has repercussion in our lives.

3.3 TOUCH

If the preceding section focused on those senses, which are properly oriented towards interior faculties, the touch involves our direct contact with the exterior world. Its culture-specific character reveals pattern of relationship we follow, and notions of community rules and mores are revealed in its usage. Touching of certain sacred things by particular kind of persons is forbidden in some instance in all cultures (Leviticus 11: 8). When community-designated persons touch others during ceremonies, divine power and energy is believed to flow from him to persons undergoing ceremony. If persons touch certain culturally and cultish prohibited animals, things and persons thought to be unclean, could be polluting. In Christian rites of passage, touching by the priests and anointing the child or the priestly candidate sets God's spirit on the child and the aspirant. God himself touches men either to change their heart (1 Samuel 10:26) or to afflict them with illness (2 Kings 15: 5).

The first passage is from the *Gospel of Mark*, chapter 8, verse 23:

> And he took the blind man by the hand, and led him out of the village; and when he had spit on his eyes and laid his hands upon him, he asked him, "Do you see anything?"

The priests and the teachers of the law usually would not touch the beggars, people afflicted with sickness and specially persons suffering from leprosy. Jesus touches these socially marginalized people in order to reveal to them the closeness of God to the poor, sick and sinners. Exercising his power to heal, Jesus' action of touching was a proclamation of a new relationship among fellow men that no human being could be unclean or in no way could his or her illness be construed as polluting. In another instance, Jesus does not rebuke the lady with twelve years of blood flow getting healed by the mere touch of him or his garment. Women who had longer discharges were barred from normal human relationships and here was a woman who dares to touch a teacher (*The New International* 3: 860). Jesus lovingly says, "Daughter, your faith has made you well; go in peace" (Luke 8: 40-48). The person who touches and the person who is touched experience power crossing from each other. Touch is always symbolical and it communicates the person's inner desires and aspirations. When Jesus heals by touch, he communicates God's power, reverses the language of purity and pollution, and strengthens the dignity of the persons in the eyes of the Lord.

3.4 TASTE

The Psalmist sings, "O taste and see that the LORD is good," (Psalms 34: 18) rendering God into food that nourishes, sustains and generates life and energy in the people.

The following passage is taken from the *Gospel of Mathew* in chapter 6, verse 24:

> Truly, I say to you, there are some standing here who will not taste death before they see the Son of man coming in his kingdom.

Accepting the word of God and living by it liberates the listeners. The preceding verses speak of the need for a person to die to one's selfishness, attaining freedom from worldly desires and possessions. So, "tasting of death" in this verse does not necessarily mean physical annihilation, rather the person who is so much immersed in this worldly affairs, totally depending on the riches of the world gradually loses the life-giving power that is granted to him. Such vivid imageries taken from the physical sensory world brings out the intensity and the urgency of the message proclaimed.

Ignatius of Loyola has written a practical treatise called *Spiritual Exercise*. The person undergoing these exercises for thirty days is proposed to apply all the five senses in imagination and draw spiritual fruits from his contemplations:

> The third point is to smell and taste in my imagination the infinite fragrance and sweetness of the divinity, and of the soul, and of its virtues, and of all else, according to the character of the person I am contemplating. And I will reflect within myself to draw spiritual profit therefrom.
>
> — Mottola 1964: 7

3.5 SMELL

Once again the sensory faculty is used as a symbol of a particular desired pattern of relationship between man and God. As a personal God, He will smell the fragrance of the sacrifices offered but only if they follow the commandments and his statutes. St. Paul calls himself as aroma of Christ (2 Corinthians 2: 15).

The five exterior senses, then, as explicated by the passages from the Bible have revelatory roles to play in acquiring the knowledge of God and His words. It must be noted that these senses are intimately linked to the human interior faculties of reason, imagination and affectivity that fashion man as a created being with the goal of coming face to face with God. If so, these senses need continual purification for they are susceptible to the immoral powers active in the world around us. Christian moral thought emphasizes the need for refining of our exterior senses in order to harmonize them with the objective of love.

4. Senses and Knowledge

Although the philosophers and moralists hold that the knowledge we attain through the senses is of lower category, they affirm their indispensability in acquiring the knowledge of temporal things. Thomas Aquinas emphatically states that human soul has no innate ideas and has to form its own ideas in dependence on sense experience. According to him, sensitive soul comprises both Five exterior senses and four interior senses: common sense, imagination, comparative judgement and memory; and the knowledge of exterior objects are apprehended, by the senses together with these faculties. However, these faculties can provide us only with knowledge of particulars and not universals. In order to relate a particular to the universal, the active intellect illumines the passive intellect that approximates the universal element in the particular object so apprehended (Copleston 2: 96-98). In discussing the senses and the sense-organs, the Christian thinkers do highlight their moral associations. Precisely because sense-organs also could divert us from the real goal of moral life and lead us into the vicious circle of sensual pleasures, the Christian morality advocates moderation in application of the senses.

Conclusion

The corporeal nature of man has been emphasized in the context of the duality debate. Nevertheless the spirit of man is spiritually corporeal; our spiritual nature desires union with transcendence and our corporeality often pulls us towards the opposite direction of material condition. It is a fluid dialectical relationship. In becoming aware of this dialectical tension, our senses could be oriented towards attaining the true happiness that includes in gaining the fruits of the spirit:

love, joy, peace, patience, kindness, goodness, faithfulness, gentleness and self-control. Further the brief analysis of sense-organs as portrayed in the Bible reveals that man in an indivisible whole; soul and body are the two dimensions of the same holistic personality. The Five sense-organs and their faculties disclose the interrelatedness that human beings experience within and without their being. Finally, seeking the subjective and objective character of this interrelatedness to oneself and to the world we encounter man's transcendent dignity as he lives in the "image and likeness" of God.

Notes

1. I am indebted to Dr. George Pattery of Vishwa Bharati University for his critical comments and suggestions while writing this paper.
2. All the quotations of Bible are taken from the Revised Standard Version.

References

Armstrong, A.H., (date not listed), *An Introduction to Ancient Philosophy.*

Baumert, Norbert L., 1996, *Woman and Man in Paul: Overcoming a Misunderstanding*, Minnesota: The Liturgical Press.

Copleston, S.J., Fredrick, 1962, *A History of Philosophy*, vol. 2 (part 1 & 2), New York: Image Books.

Isherwood, Lisa & Elizabeth Stuart, 1998, *Introducing Body Theology*, Sheffield: Sheffield Academic Press.

John Paul II, 1981, *Original Unity of Man and Woman: Catechesis on the Book of Genesis*, Boston: Daughters of St. Paul.

Mottola, Anthony (tr.), 1964, *The Spiritual Exercise of St. Ignatius*, New York: Image Books.

Sacramentum mundi: An Encyclopaedia of Theology: vol. I, ed. Karl Rahner et. al., 1969, London: Burns & Oates.

The New International Dictionary of New Testament Theology in 5 vols., ed. Colin Brown et al., 1978, Michigan: Zonderman Publishing House.

The Interpreter's Dictionary of the Bible: An Ilustrated Encyclopedia in 4 vols., ed. Geroge Arthur Buttrick et al., 1962, New York: Abingdon Press.

Part II
Science and Society

13

Santal Perception of Organs and the Senses

Onkar Prasad

THERE are Five sense-organs, i.e. the eye, the ear, the nose, the tongue and the skin, through which man and animal become aware of what is happening around them. Correspondingly, there is "fivefoldness": seeing, hearing, smell, taste and touch — the Five powers of the body — by which one receives knowledge of things around (Hornby, 1989: 1151). Receiving knowledge through the Five senses relate to perception, which in itself is an act of culture. This paper attempts to study the Santal perception of sense-organs and the senses, "they being not only means of understanding and perceiving physical phenomena but also avenues for the transmission of cultural values" (Herzfeld, 2004: 240). The data have been collected from the Santals* of Balipara, Pearson Palli and Koet Pukur Danga, hamlets of the Bolpur-Sriniketan Block of Birbhum district in West Bengal.

The Santals, like other population groups of India, classify the sense-organs into Five types — *met'* (eye), *muk'* (nose), *lutur* (ear), *alan* (tongue) and *harta* (skin). Also senses into Five

* The Santals are a tribe of Proto-Australoid origin, inhabiting predominantly in the contiguous areas of the states of Jharkhand, Orissa and West Bengal. They speak Santali, a language of the Austric speech family, and subsist mainly on agriculture, with some marginal dependence on hunting and gathering.

types — *nel* (sight), *anjom* (hearing), *so* (smell), *sebel* (taste) and *jotet'* (touch), as discussed below:

Met' and Nel: The Eye and the Sight

The eye is an apparatus for "seeing" things around the world. Following the Santal riddle, it is said to be present everywhere (*hani honḍe nuu nonḍ*, i.e. it is here, it is there).

THE EYE CATEGORIES

The Santals classify human eyes more extensively. For example, *lundu met'* raised eye, *poa' met'* big but round eye, *pusi met'* (cat's eye), *kokor met'* (owl's eye), *kara met'* (buffalo's eye), *thuia met'* (sunken eye), *tut met'* (protruding eye), *pond met'* (white or pale eye), *arak' met'* (red eye), *tra or ghote met'* (squint eye), *kurit' met'* (kite's eye), *pincar met'* peacock's eye, *pansakam met'* betel leaf-shaped eye), *rol met'* (myrobalan-shaped eye), *hako met'* (fish's eye), etc. The ritual of *cokhdon* (eye-sacrifice) is also observed when a family member dies. If not done, the deceased member may appear regularly. It is believed that a person having *lundu met'* possesses power of the *bonga* (spirit). *Kokor met'* or *pusi met'* is associated with a witch or a sorcerer. *Haku met'* is generally believed to be cruel by nature, and so on.

THE SIGHT — AUSPICIOUS AND INAUSPICIOUS

The Santals classify *nel* (sight) mainly into two types: *mette nel* (seeing through eyes) and *kukmute nel* (seeing in dreams). In day-to-day life, they attach much value to these two types of sight in terms of *bhagi* (auspicious) and *baric* (inauspicious). For an auspicious work, if they pay different visits, omens are carefully taken into consideration. A man carrying an axe or a mattock, someone cutting wood, a branch falling from a tree, or ashes being carried are taken as ominous. These actions, in various ways, are connected with death. For example the axe is used for cutting wood at a funeral, the mattock is used for digging a grave, the branch of a tree may swell on pyre, and ashes are what the dead becomes. The good omens are identified with a pot full of water, a herd of cattle, corpse, someone washing clothes, and an empty pot to be filled. A full pot is good, because it shows that the purpose of journey is about to be fulfilled. A corpse is also good since death is temporarily appeased, and the man's destiny of death is accomplished. Clean clothes are auspicious, because all the dirt has been washed away. These omens do not *necessarily* make or mar a proposal, but they are not without importance. Often, they seem subconsciously to affect the decision while occasionally they are even "staged" in order to deter a party from proceeding with its plans (Archer, 1974: 173). Similarly, in dreams, seeing the falling stars is taken as a good omen, and vulture entering a house with a bone as a bad omen.

For the Santals, highly ominous is the "evil-eye" possessed by their women. There is also a belief that an abnormal birth of male or female may lead to have the "evil-eye." The evil-eye is considered to be the source of all troubles and mischiefs. It can bring ruin to a person, destroy his household members, as also domestic animals and crops. This belief has its root in a myth describing how the Santal women learnt witchcraft, in the guise of men, from Maran Buru, one of the presiding spirits of the Santals and thereby they are imbued with strange mysterious powers to the extent that they can bring out *the heart of a man to fry and eat*. In order to counter the bad effect of the evil-eye of the women the tribal society has developed some rituals. When a Santal woman is pregnant, her husband cannot eat the head of an animal. If he does not observe this taboo, he would fail to see the very type of animals during its prey. When a child is in a mother's womb, the mid-wife performs *met' halan*, the ritual of "lifting the eye," to avoid miscarriage or physical deformity of the child. The same ritual is performed at birth to protect both the mother and the child from evil influence. During marriage, rituals like the *cumaura* (kissing) and *parchau* are also performed to ward off the evil-eye (Troisi, 1978: 222-224).

THE SIGHT-PERCEPTION OF COLOUR

The colour is an aspect of sight. The Santals classify colour into six categories: *pond* (white), *sasan'* (yellow), *herak'* (speckled), *hende* (black), *hariar* (green), and *arak'* (red). In their perception, *pond* (white) is pure and auspicious. So is yellow, which is their most favourite one. *Herak'* (speckled) is favourite to Jaher' Era, one of their presiding spirits, to whom the Santals sacrifice a fowl of speckled colour. *Hende* (black) is inauspicious, as it is feared by them. *Hariar* (green) is pleasant to the Santals, but *arak* (red) is inauspicious, as it represents death, and hence avoided.

Lutur and Anjom: The Ear and the Hearing

THE EAR CATEGORIES

The Santals classify the ear into the types like *kaṭic* (small), *dhalka* (broad), *hatak'* (winnowing fan), *sugut* (mongoose), *keruapatka* (twisted), *setak* (dog's ear), *thuni* (a man having this type of ear cannot hear immediately), *etan* (a man having this type of ear has a tendency to hear everything), *buci* (an ear having cut marks), etc. Among the Santals, the ear is treated as a symbol of prestige. Anything wrong-done is thought to have "cut the ear." They say *kuri gidre disam hor talare luture get' acukidiyan* (the work, which the boy and the girl have done, has led to cut the ear in the eyes of the people of the country). In Hindi-speaking area, the expression is "cut the nose" (*nāka kaṭanā*), that is to lose prestige."

THE HEARING CATEGORIES

Hearing is the sense with which sound is perceived. The Santals classify sounds of different origins: humans, animals and other material objects, into three major categories: *saḍe, araṅ* and *rak.'* The term *saḍe* is used to refer, and to include, those sounds which are produced as a result of stroke or collision. The term *araṅ* is used to refer and to include those sounds which are produced by human beings, be that the speech sound or the melodic sound. The rhythmic as well tonal sounds, produced by various musical instruments, are also included under this category.

The term *rak'* is used to refer to those sounds which are produced by animals, birds and insects. The painful cry of human being is also under this category. Further, there are some calls of certain animals which are not included in either of the categories, viz. the call of the cow, the calf, the buffalo, etc.

From the Santal classification of sound, it is clear that hearing is inherent, the basic principle of differentiation as well as unification, under all things of the universe.

THE HEARING AUSPICIOUS AND INAUSPICIOUS

The Santals believe that hearing of some kinds of sounds are auspicious, and some inauspicious. For example, hearing of the call of the bird *pio* near a house is taken as auspicious, as it indicates the coming of the guest in the house. Hearing of untimely call of the cock, between evening meal and midnight, is taken as inauspicious as it indicates entering of an evil spirit in the house that may cause harm to a member of the household. In order to ward off the evil spirit, the villagers trace out the house, kill the cock, and eat it next morning.

Muk' and So: The Nose and the Smell

The sensory organ through which smell of various types is received comes under the category *muk'* (nose). In Santal riddles, its depth is compared with the bottom of a king's well, i.e. one which is not easily visible (*raja kuinen yunteak dare keak'*), or with the underneath (*patalreak kuin neltie daream*) for the sake of fun.

THE NOSE CATEGORIES

The Santals classify nose into such types as *doc' muk'* (parrot-nose) *bhinti muk'* (sickle-nose), *mota muk'* (nose which is not sensitive to smell), *dondor muk'* (cave like nose), *cepre muk'* (flat nose), *dumbu muk'* (round nose), *daria muk'* (insensible nose), etc. These varied categories of nose generally occur in *sogoe* (jokes) to refer to different girls, during dance performance. The Santals also have a practice of piercing nose, as a proof of their Santal identity.

THE SMELL CATEGORIES

The Santals classify the smell of various types, received through nose, broadly into two categories: *sahao* (tolerable) and *ban sahao* (intolerable), also classify it in terms of *bhagi* (pleasant) and *baric* (unpleasant). The *bhagi* is further classified into six categories: *herem* (sweet), *tasi* (pungent), *jojo* (sour), *siric* (scented), *sondhar* (flavour of fried corns) and *morot'* (flavour emitted at the time of singeing of an animal). As the Santals believe, *sondha so* is favourite to their spirits and therefore fried seeds of fenugreek are offered to appease them. They classify *baric so* further into five types — *rongo* (smell of burnt curry), *dhuarata* (smell of smoke), *hiluat'* (intolerable smell of half-rotten food), *jojo* (sourly smell but bad) and *sea* (smell of a fully rotten food). This smell is considered very poisoning.

The Santals believe that smell helps in judging the quality of food and drink. In addition to these, they do not include the smell of plants, fruits and flowers in either of the categories, and identify it in reference to each of them. For example *sakam so, bili so,* etc. (for detail see Bhattacharyya 2000: 37-38).

Alan and Sebel: The Tongue and the Taste

The sensory organ which mainly determines the taste is *alan* (tongue). In Santal riddles this organ is compared with the temperament of the cat, bear or tiger, e.g. *kudum kurit' kurit' pusi menked jojo ho jojogi nimḥo harhadgi, cinima heremge pusi do okoe*? (The tamarind is sour, the margosa leaf is bitter, sugar is sweet, where is the cat?); *kultarup' menkeda hakumai siriogi, jilma sebelgi, bulunma rahangi, kultarup do okoe*? (The bear and the tiger say, the fish is tasty, the meat is tasteful, the salt is salty, where are the bear and the tiger?)

THE TONGUE CATEGORIES

The Santals classify the tongue in such types as *jilin* (long), *capra* (flat or broad), *kabra* (spotted), *mota* (thick) and *sagat* (rough which the witch generally has).

THE TASTE CATEGORIES

The Santals classify *sebel* (taste) mainly with reference to food. They classify taste of food items, other than rice-beer into twelve types: *gargat'* (hot and pungent), *sorom* (good), *sondhar* (taste of fried fenugreek), *raham* (salted), *kasa* (astringent), *lunjer* (taste of smooth objects), *jojo* (sour), *comkoc'* (mixed taste of sour and sweet), *herem* (sweet) *jhal* (hot), *harhat'* (bitter) and *jolat rongo* (taste of food stuck to the vessel during cooking). It may be noted that they prepare rice-gruel with margosa leaves to offer to the ancestral spirits, and also eaten by all villagers to get ritually purified, to achieve normal status, after the family and the villagers have been defiled at the birth of a child.

The Santals classify the taste of rice-bear into three types, *herem* (sweet but not favourite), *tasil* (hot, pungent and tasteful commonly taken and served to the guests), and *gargat tasil* (very hot and pungently aromatic served only to the honourable guests). They also classify *sabajom* (tasteless food) into two types — one which does not taste but can be eaten and *payarsabe,* i.e. one which is totally tasteless and cannot be eaten (for details see Bhattacharyya, 2000: 38-39).

Harta and Jotet': The Skin and the Touch

The Santals use the term *harta* for skin as a sensory organ. They use the term *jotet* for touch, a valued socio-religious code of behaviour. Ritually, the night before a festival begins, the village-priest becomes abstinent. He sleeps on the ground on a mat alone, because before initiating a ritual the sacrificer must not have any physical relation with his wife. Socially, the relatives among whom touch is permitted fall in a particular kind of relationship known as *landa sagai* (laugh relationship). This includes the *gorom ba* and the *gorom budhi* (the grandparents) and their *gorom kora* and *gorom kuri* (the grandchildren), *mama, mami* and *bhagna, bhagnain* (maternal uncle and aunt and their nephew and niece), *bala kora* and *bala kuri* (husband's younger brother and sister). Anybody having relation of *karam dar* (friend) can also touch each other. Besides all those boys and girls who are not agnates must also be permitted to do so. But the social rules prohibit the Santals to touch the following relatives.

ajhnarea	:	A girl's husband and her elder sister.
bala kora	:	A girl's mother and her husband's father.
bala kuri	:	A boy's mother and his wife's father.
tala bahu, hopon bahu	:	Younger brother's wife.
bahonharea	:	A girl's husband and her elder brother's wife and her husband's elder brother.

Social rule is observed for avoiding physical relation. If violated, Santal is subject to penalties and punishment.

Touch is also a means of bringing physical intimacy between the members of the opposite sex. The pre-marital sex is socially permitted, except within the members of the same clan. Festive occasion, especially the *sohrae,* encourages this. In a meeting, the *jog manjhi* (the guardian of morality) suggests the villagers "to put twelve wads of cotton in their ears, and to see and hear nothing for five days." He also instructs the boys and the girls to take "ripe" but not "unripe."*

Observation of the Foreign Scholars

The entire period of the celebration of *sohrae* is characterized by "every unimaginable kind of debauchery" (Man, 1983: 56). A general saturnalia of drunkenness and sexual licence prevails. Chastity is in abeyance for the time and all unmarried persons may indulge in promiscuous intercourse. (Risley, 1981: 233). "The whole period is characterized by its freedom from traditional morality. The rules of avoidance are treated lightly and many liberties are taken with members of the opposite sex" (Culshaw, 1949: 112-13).

Summing Up

From the data available it is observed that Santals broadly classify senses into two categories — auspicious and inauspicious — in terms of effects produced on their life. The sight which the Santals believe to be the most inauspicious, is the *evil-eye of the women*, held responsible for bringing ruins to an individual's life. The power of the evil-eye seems to be the basis of the genesis of witchcraft, an institution as well as of the emergence of some rituals like *met' halan, parachau* and *cumaura* in the Santal society.

Colour is also an important aspect of vision. The Santals show more preference for the yellow colour, and treat the black and the red as ominous which symbolize fear and death, respectively.

---

* The *jog majhi* while uttering *bakher* (an invocatory statement) during the *sohorai* cautions the adult male members of the village not to use *jhanti jhinga* (the term figuratively used to refer to a girl whose marriage has been fixed), *dodo jhinga* (aged women) and *bale jhinga* (unripe girls) and even the girl who has been engaged. (*sutom teko tolaka, cerec' teko gutukaka onakodo alope Sidak* — Personal communication with Tarachand Murmu.

Like *sight*, the Santals classify *hearing* into two categories: auspicious and inauspicious. These categories serve as a guiding principle in organizing their life-activities. Further, the Santals classify *smell* broadly into two: pleasant and unpleasant in relation to food, and other items. The item having *sondha* smell is believed to be favourite to their spirits, and hence considered as an *odour* of sanctity. So is the case with the item having *sondha taste*. Of the food items, rice-gruel prepared with margosa leaves, that taste bitter, is believed to remove impurity and hence drunk by the members of a household and the village, after both having been polluted at the birth of a child.

Touch serves a twofold function in the Santal society: one as a ritual code and another as a social code. As a ritual code, it prohibits the Santal priest to have any physical touch with his wife, before performing any ritual on a festive occasion. As a social code, it prohibits to touch some kin members, but at the same time it allows the boys and the girls to indulge in sexual relation to the extremity, specially during the post-harvest festival, symbolizing the ploughing of the earth for regaining fertility, after it has been made barren during harvest. In terms of touch, however, the Santals may be labelled as sensualists.

In brief it may be said that in Santal perception *sight* is associated with witchcraft, *ear* with prestige, *taste* and *smell* with sanctity and *touch* with sensuality.

References

Archer, W.G., 1947, *The Hill of Flutes: Life, Love and Poetry in Tribal India*, New Delhi: S. Chand and Co. (Pvt.) Ltd.

Bhattacharya, Indrani, 2000, *Santal Knowledge of Food: Comparative Study in Rural and Semi-urbanized Areas of Birbhum*, Unpublished Ph.D. thesis.

Culshaw, W.J., 1949, *Tribal Heritage: A Study of the Santals*, London: Lutherworth Press.

Herzfeld, Michael, 2004, "Senses in Anthropology," in *Anthropology: Theoretical Practice in Culture and Society*, pp. 240-53, Rawat Publications.

Hornby, A.S., 1989, *Oxford Advanced Learner's Dictionary of Current English*, Oxford University Press (4th edn.).

Man, E.G., 1983, *Sonthalia and the Sonthals*, Calcutta: Geo Wyaman and Co. (Reprint of 1867).

Risley, H.H., 1981, *The Tribes and Castes of Bengal*, vol. II, Calcutta: Firma K.K. Mukhopadhyay (Reprint of 1891).

Troisi, J., 1979, *Tribal Religion: Religious Beliefs and Practices Among the Santals*, New Delhi: Manohar Publishers.

14

Function of the Sense-Organs in the Snake-Catching Technology

Sanghamitra Pal

THE present paper based on an empirical study among the Sapure Mal — the snake-charmers of Bhedia, Burdwan District, West Bengal, seeks to explore some aspects of the senses in the snake-catching technology.

The Sapure Mal is one of the sub-castes of the caste Mal. The word "Mal" is derived from the compound words *malla kṣatriya* which means "wrestler or soldier caste" (Singh: 1993). They have been classified differently by different ethnographers. Whereas Risley (1981) classifies them into 12 more sub-caste groups, Singh (1993) classifies them into four sub-caste groups. The latter classification holds true in case of Burdwaṅ. In this district the sub-castes of the Mal are — (i) Rajbanshi Mal who are cultivators; (ii) Chitrakar Mal who earn their livelihood by idol-making; (iii) Patua Mal who are idol-makers and scroll painters and also show scroll in different fairs and villages, etc.; and (iv) Sapure Mal or Bede Mal who earn their livelihood by snake-catching and charming.

The Sapure Mal is considered having lower social status than the other three *"Thaks"* (sub-castes) due to their profession of snake-catching and charming and also for their semi-nomadic habit.

The Sapure are distributed in rural areas of all districts of West Bengal, except Purulia. They are also found in some villages of Burdwan district. The author, therefore, selected the village Bhedia for intensive fieldwork due to their maximum concentration in that village.

Previously, as observed by Ray (1966), the Sapure were nomadic people. They are, however, leading a settled life for two generations. In course of my fieldwork, it was observed that the Sapure people in this area lead a semi-nomadic life, as they have to move from one place to another for snake catching and charming. In fact, the catching of snakes has been a way of their life.

The snake catching and charming is a profession of a very specialized nature. This profession which is very dangerous for life, needs specially senses-oriented skill. In this paper an attempt has been made to deal with the sensory experiences of the Sapure Mal, which they make use of in the technology of snake-catching.

Classification of the Snake

The Sapure call the snake as *moshel.* They classify it into two broad categories, i.e. (A) Poisonous snakes (*moshel* with *naji*), and (B) Non-poisonous snakes (*moshel* without *naji*). Poison is called *naji* by the Sapure. Further these poisonous snakes are broadly categorized into two types in terms of hood, i.e. — "snakes with hood" and "snakes without hood." According to my informants Dilip Mal, Khalon Mal and others, there are three varieties of snakes that have hoods, i.e. — (a) *gokhura* or *khoris,* (b) *sankhachoor,* (c) *keoute.* The *gokhura* or *khoris,* that has hood, is further classified into three types: *metho, dudhe* and *tentule.* The *methokhoris* is identified in terms of their usual habitat. This snake lives in the fields (*maths*). The *Dudhekhoris* is milky (*dudh*) in complexion while the *tentulekhoris* has tamarind (*tentul*) complexion.

The snakes without hoods are broadly categorized into two types in terms of their colour. They are *chitti* and *sankhini*. The *chitti* is called *kalachi* by the Sapure because of black (*kalo*) spots on its body.

According to the habitat, the *chitti* is again classified into three types. For instance, the snake that habitually lives in the field is called *domanachitti*. The *chitti* that lives in the straw roof (*chal*) is identified as *chalchitti*. In the same manner, *chitti* that lives in the hill is called *paharichitti* (Python). The Sapure, however, do not consider the *paharichitti* as poisonous. The *sankhini* or *shekamuti* or *rajsap* is a poisonous snake and is called *goli* by the Sapure. This snake is very long and its body is covered by alternatively black and yellow coloured band and the tail region is rough.

The non-poisonous snakes (*moshel* without *naji*) are broadly classified into three types, such as *kalnagini*, *borha* and *dhamma*. The *kalnagini* is of dark complexion and habitually lives on trees and it is also called as *vichut* by the Sapure. The *borha* is further categorized in terms of its normal habitat and temperament. For instance, the *borha* that prefers sand (*bali*) pit for its normal habitat is identified as *baliborha* (Sandboa), while that living in the grass (*ghas*) is called *gheso borha*. The snakes that live on trees (*gachh*), are identified as *gechho borha* (Pit Viper). The *chandro borha* (Russell's Viper) is called as *josur* by the Sapure for its aggressive attitude. This snake is also identified for its fast jumping motion. To them, the *chandro borha* is, however, a poisonous snake in the group of *borha*. The *dhamma* is also locally called as *rona* signifying its habit of running fast.

Habit

The Sapure believe that most of the snakes are harmless and do not normally attack any other animal. The poisonous snakes generally possess hoods and make hissing and whistling sounds when they go to attack the enemy. They move out

The Classification of Snakes as Understood from the Sapure is Furnished below in a Tabular Form

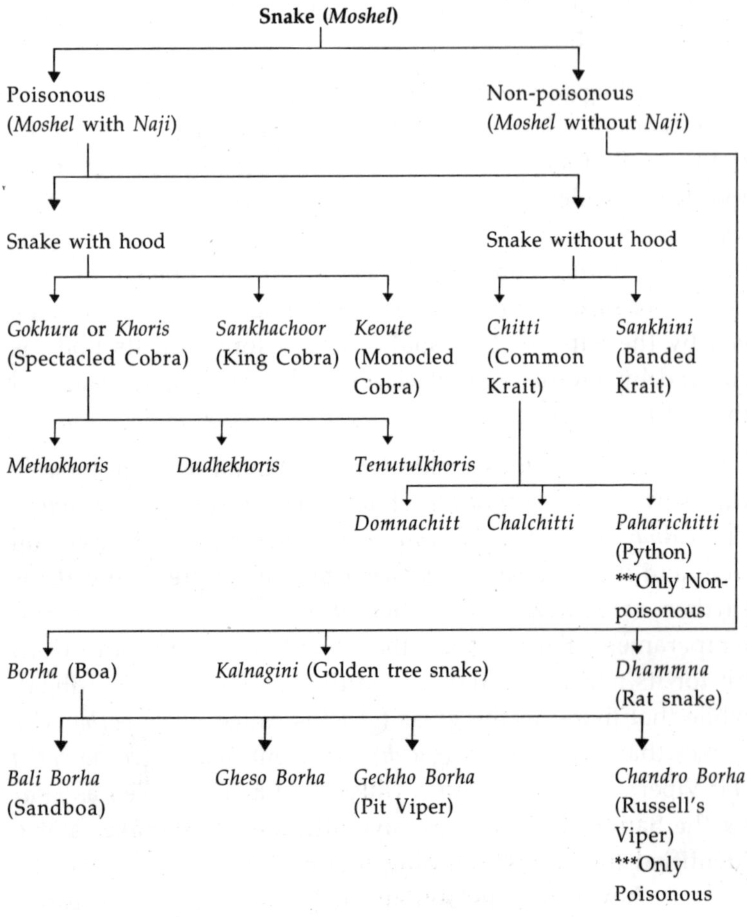

early in the morning and early in the evening. According to the Sapure, the poisonous snakes come back to their shelter after sunrise at about 7 a.m. and the Sapure go to catch the snakes around 8 a.m. because their body spots are clearly visible in the sunlight. The the Sapure, non-poisonous snakes possess no hoods and move at any time in day.

In course of day-to-day observation, it is learnt that the snakes are habitually timid in nature but during mating seasons they become aggressive. After laying eggs or giving birth, the *nāgin* (female snake) becomes very alert and at that time she tries to protect her eggs from any enemy.

The Sapure distinguish different types of snakes by their habit. In course of their day-to-day experience, I have learnt that a *gokhura* (spectacled cobra) snake habitually expands its hood, stops still and slowly moves its hood before jumping upon its prey.

Methokhoris is a variety of spectacled cobras. This snake is more aggressive than any other variety of the *khoris* or *gokhura. Dudhekhoris,* another variety of the spectacled cobra is also aggressive in nature. It moves with whistling sound primarily to frighten men and other animals on its way. Normally, the snake does not attack without provocation. On the other hand, the *keoute* (monocled cobra) is very aggressive and the intensity of attack is high.

The *sankhochoor* (king cobra) is highly poisonous and very aggressive in nature. It can stand perpendicularly erect by balancing on its tail, and attacks most other animals from a long distance. The *chandro borha* (Russell's viper) is the only poisonous snake in the group of *borha.* The snakes can make long jumps from one place to another. For this habit of the snake, the Sapure normally do not catch the *chandro borha. Gheso borha* is another variety of *borha,* which is non-poisonous. It jumps slowly from one place to another. According to the Sapure, this snake has a very keen vision.

The *dhamma* (rat snake) is a non-poisonous snake. For its very fast body motion, this snake is called *rona* by the Sapure. According to them, *rona* means "the one that runs fast."

Habitat: The Identification of Catching Sites

From their traditional knowledge, the Sapure know that the snakes normally live in rat holes. If the ground is levelled and soil of the trail at the entrance of the hole looks bright in sunlight then the Sapure become almost certain that the snake has recently entered into the hole. Moreover, by smelling the soil and observing body spot left on the soil, the Sapure ascertain the kind of snake present in the hole. It may be mentioned that if they get fishy smell and oval-shaped body spots on the ground, they are sure of the presence of some poisonous snakes in the hole. Non-poisonous snakes leave square-shaped body spots on the ground.

They also know that some snakes normally live in ponds and others in water pools. Some of the snakes also prefer to live in marshy lands besides the water pools. According to my informants the snakes living in water pools are generally non-poisonous. They say that these snakes do not lay eggs since incubation is not possible in the cold surrounding of the water pools. Instead these snakes give birth to the young ones in the water pools. Different types of *borha* (Boa), viz. Sand Boa, Pit Viper, Russell's Viper, and Banded Krait fall in this category.

Mating

The Sapure say that the Bengali month *Jaistha* (May-June) is considered the mating season of the snakes. During this mating period, the snakes become aggressive and at that time toxicity of venom is comparatively high. During this time, the Sapure also become very alert and cautious at catching snakes and they do not move individually for snake-catching. According to my informants, each variety of snakes mates with its own species. A hoodless snake does not mate with a snake possessing hood. They also say that a poisonous snake does not mate with a non-poisonous snake.

Birth

From their day-to-day observation, the Sapure, however, identify that the male snakes possess comparatively broad face and thick tail region than the female snakes. The Sapure say that the *nāgin* (female snakes) lays eggs after the *Dasher* of *Āṣaḍha* (the tenth day of Bengali month *Āṣāḍha,* June-July. When a *nāgin* carries eggs, her face becomes reddish in colour and after laying of eggs the reddish colour disappears. The Sapure also say that the period between mating and new-born is about two months.

According to a Sapure, a *keoute* (monocled cobra) may lay 16 eggs at a time. The hatching of the eggs continues for a period of about 15 days. At that time, the mother snake becomes too weak to move, and toxicity of venom also comes down. After 15 days, new young snakes are born. During this period snake-catching is very difficult because the mother snakes become very aggressive and she always protects her young ones.

Death

The snake is a cold-blooded animal. In extreme cold and hot weather it cannot survive. My informants Dulal Mal and others could not tell the accurate life span of snakes. From their regular observation, it is estimated by them that snakes can stay for a long time in the basket during winter season. The snakes during winter are normally kept in the baskets, and often warmed in the sun to protect them from cold.

General Observation

In course of my fieldwork among the Sapure Mal of the village of Bhedia, it has been observed that the senses like sight, hearing, smell and touch are most important in the snake-catching technology. Almost all the male members of the Sapure community know the art of snake-catching and charming. The Sapure, since childhood, are accustomed to live with snakes in their houses. Since then they overcome fear by carrying *jhapi* (snakes basket) and also touching the snakes in their houses.

Although there are no written records about their knowledge and skill of snake-catching and charming, however, the Sapure learn them through participation in the art of snake catching since childhood. They, by sensory experience, can identify different types of snakes and also perceive their nature easily. The Sapure believe that the snake-catching activity mainly depends on keen observation and the technique of catching. Moreover, the Sapure create various mystic activities around their world of snakes by which they live in a world of dynamic isolation.

References

Ray, Niharranjan, 1996, *Bangalir Ethihas* (*Adiparba; Beng.*), Lakhok Samobaya Samiti, Calcutta.

Risley, H.H., 1981, *The Tribes and Castes of Bengal* (*Ethnographic Glossary*), vol. II, Calcutta: Firma K.L.M. Mukhopadhyay.

Singh, K.S., 1993, *People of India, National Series,* vol. II, *The Scheduled Castes,* O'Neil Brein, Oxford University Press.

15

Animal Behaviour During Natural Disaster

And Their Role for the Welfare of Mankind

Saroj Kr. Pyne
Gautam Samanta

Introduction

SENSATIONS generally are the result of different impulses from stimuli that eventually reach a conscious level in the cerebral cortex. However, some different impulses may function in somatic reflexes without ever reaching the level of consciousness. Special senses include smell, sight, taste, hearing and equilibrium. Organic sensations include, among others, hunger, thirst, the sensation of bladder-fullness, and sexual sensations. Other sensations not classified above include touch, pressure, cold, heat, pain, proprioception and visceral sensations.

Special feature of sensory organ in animals' proprioception, also called muscle sense, indicates to the animal the relative positions of various parts of the body without using its eyes, which is important for animals for walking, running, fighting and grazing. The sense of smell is mediated by the olfactory nerve, development of which varies from species to species. It is well developed in the dog but poorly developed in man. Walker in his research described that canines' sense of smell is 10,000 to 100,000 times superior to that of human beings.

Dog's olfactory senses are so sensitive that they are said to be able to smell fear — that it's possible they could pick up on chemical changes in the air before an earthquake.

Case Study of Animal's Response

In Khao Lak, 50 miles north of Phuket along Thailand's western coast, a dozen elephants giving tourist rides began trumpeting hours before the December 26, 2004 tsunami, when a 9.0 magnitude quake fractured the ocean floor.

At the hard-hit Yala National Park in Sri Lanka, stunned wildlife. Officials reported that hundreds of elephants, leopards, tigers, wild boars, deers, water buffaloes, monkeys, etc. had escaped unscathed. Seismologists have sophisticated instruments that can measure quake factors during and after the fact, but experts admit no one can predict exactly when one will happen, whereas certain animals have a kind of sensory hard-wiring that can detect earthquake ahead of time. This might be replicated in man-made instruments.

Reports on animals's "Sixth Sense" in detecting hurricanes, earthquakes, tsunamis and volcanic eruptions long before the earth starts shaking go back centuries — Rats racing from building, sparrows taking flight in flocks, dogs howling incessantly, etc. It is an impressive track record though anecdotal. An eyewitness to the phenomenon, a Danish man stated "dogs were running away up to the hill tops long before we even realized about December 26 tsunami" when he was staying in Ao Sane Beach, north of Phuket. Science is iffy on a subject that, for obvious reasons, is difficult to replicate in a laboratory. And there are always explanations and theories that mitigate the mystery of the anecdotes.

Some scientists are looking for explanation of why some species behave strangely before catastrophes, by correlating the animals' sensory abilities with microscopic and invisible sensory stimuli.

Grant says, "I don't know if I would call this a sixth sense so much as a better sense." He explained, most animals know that when the ground starts to shake something is wrong, animal's sensory physiology — supersensitive to sound, temperature, touch, vibration, electrostatic and chemical activity and magnetic fields — gives them a head start in the days and hours before natural calamities.

George Pararas-Carayannis, a former Oceanographer and geophysicist of University of Hawaii, who leads the Tsunami Society, realized that a lot of animals have sensory organs that detect these micro-tremors and micro-changes that are not be possible by human beings. It is a sensitivity that we humans don't have. But animals, through millions of years of evolution, have developed it and survive as a species.

John Caprio, Professor of Biological Sciences, described that many fishes are sensitive to low-frequency vibrations and detect tremors long before humans. A bull-head catfish detects magnitude-2 earthquakes.

Lynette Hart, Scientist of animal behaviour, noted that elephants felt the quake in their feet and trunks, and also they can figure out what direction the stimulus is coming from, how strong it is and what evasive action to take.

Species of birds, dogs, elephants, tigers and other animals can detect "infra sound," says psychobiologist James Walker, of frequencies in the range of 1-3 hertz, in comparison to humans' 100-200 hertz range. They are sensitive to such a low frequency range that most people would'nt call it sound any more.

However, Ben Hart, Professor of Animal Physiology, told that animal's pre-quake behaviour is inconsistent. It is a fact that animals can sense anything, including very minor changes that happen before earthquakes, but there is so much background noise during an earthquake, that it is unclear what stimuli the animals are reacting to.

Thus, it may be concluded that such responses of animals may be helpful to control huge losses due to natural disaster in near future. We are also hopeful that detection of bladder and prostate cancer might be possible through trained dogs which is under investigation.

References

Frandson, R.D., 1965, *Anatomy and Physiology of Farm Animals,* Philadelphia: Lea and Febiger, pp. 102-16.

Ghosh, Lakshmi B., "Can We Learn From Animals"?, *The Hindu,* 23rd June, 2005.

Khaolak, *Animals of the Tsunami* — "Animals Have a Sixth Sense," Thailand, *Reuters*, 5th January, 2005.

"Learning From the Tsunami", *The Ecologist,* 1st January, 2005.

Loura Dusoford, "A Sixth Sense for Tsunamis"?, *Radio Netherlands,* January 2005.
"Did Sixth Sense Save the Animals", *Mind Power News,* No. 72, 7th January, 2005.

Maryann, Mott, "Did Animals Sense Tsunami was Coming"?, *National Geographic News*, 4th January, 2005.

"Scientists Investigate Wildlife's Possible Warning Systems": Don Oldenburg, *Dawn-International,* 10th January, 2005.

16

Plant Response to External Stimuli

Somasish Ghosh Dastidar
Manojit Debnath

In our day-to-day life we come across many external stimuli to which we respond externally as well as internally. External manifestation of stimuli is exemplified by repulsive withdrawal of a body part on contact with a hot object or automatic closing of the eyelids on exposure to bright light. Internal response to stimuli is exemplified by excessive sweating during summer to bring down body temperature or other physiological alterations. But what about the most abundant greeny neighbour around us ! Do they also respond to external stimuli?

We thank humbly a gem of a scientist, our own Sir Jagadish Chandra Bose for unraveling this mystery. Yes plants also respond and that had been recorded by Seismograph (also another wonder work of the genius).

One defining characteristic of life is an ability to respond to stimuli. Adaptive organisms respond to stimuli because it leads to longevity and survival. Animals have nerves and muscles; **plants respond by growth patterns**. Two significant plant movements given prime importance are — (a) **Tropic** and (b) **Nastic** movement.

Tropism is plant growth towards or away from a directional stimulus. Direction, here, is important as the stimulus comes from only a single direction instead of many. Growth toward a stimulus is a positive tropism; growth away from a stimulus is negative tropism. By differential growth (unequal growth), one side elongates faster, resulting in curving towards or away from a stimulus. Three well known tropisms are identified as per the source of stimuli. **Phototropism** is growth of plants in response to light, stem shows positive phototropism where roots lead the other way. **Gravitotropism** (often placed along with geotropism) is response to earth's gravity, roots demonstrate positive gravitotropism whereas the shoots generally respond negatively. **Thigmotropism** is unequal growth due to touch (e.g. coiling of tendrils around a pole).

In contrast to tropism, nastic movements are independent of the direction of the stimulus. Seismonastic movements result from touch, shaking or thermal stimulation. This response takes a second or two, is due to loss of turgor pressure within cells. When a *Mimosa pudica* (*lajjābaṭī*) leaf is touched, leaflets fold because petioles droop. At the base of such leaves is a thickening called **pulvinus** where turgor pressures can drop suddenly. This is caused by exit of potassium ions out of the cells; water also comes out through osmosis resulting in a drop in turgor pressure.

A single stimulus such as hot needle can cause leaves to respond. The venus flytrap has three sensitive hairs at the base of the trap. When touched by an insect, an impulse type stimulus triggers the trap to close. Turgor pressure leaf cells propel the trap.

It is possible for a plant to respond to the vibrations accompanying sounds. We emphasize again that while there are responses to sound/vibration in plants, there is no controlled study published on the musical taste or music appreciation by plants in reputable journals. One plant that responds to sound-induced vibration is *Mimosa pudica,* also known as the "sensitive plant." Vibrations induce electrical signals across the leaflets of this plant, and cells at the base of the leaflets respond to these action potentials osmotically. This response results in a sharp change in the turgor pressure in these pulvinus cells, and that pressure change, in turn, results in the folding of the blade at the pulvinus. Another pulvinus at the base of the petiole may also respond if the vibration is severe enough. This kind of response is another example of **seismonasty.** How would this plant respond in terms of growth if its leaves were kept closed by constant vibration? If you think very long about photosynthesis in leaves as the driving force for growth, you will realize that continuous leaflet closure would *inhibit* rather than stimulate the growth of the plant. Indeed loud sounds (vibrations really) have been reported to negatively impact plant growth (reference below).

In a somewhat contrasting style this article was published in *Deccan Herald*. "Everyday, orchids growing in "Flora Exotica," the orchidarium located on the India Carbon Limited (ICL) campus, listen to songs by Lata Mangeshkar, Jagjit Singh and Pankaj Udhas. ICL, producing petroleum coke in Guwahati, is spread over three hectares. The orchid plantation area is dotted with sound boxes attached to a hi-fi music system of 1000 watts. Every morning (6.00 a.m. to 9.00 a.m.) and evening (3.00 p.m. to 5.00 p.m.), the sound system plays devotional songs, ghazals, religious chants and instrumental music for the orchids. "Orchids, like other plants, love music. Music is essential to their growth. The vibration in it helps in the growth of buds," says Dr K.N. Bhagawati, former head of Plant Pathology at Assam Agricultural University. Dr. Bhagawati has been associated with ICL for 12 years now. Music was introduced in the orchidarium in 1997. Research indicates that plants thrive if soothing music is played in the background. However, they shrivel and die if exposed to loud music. Almost 30 years ago, a woman teaching at Colorado

University conducted experiments on plants and concluded that they thrive on classical music — particularly the sitar. Recently, a Japanese company created a gadget, "Plantone," that gauges the electrical activity in plants. It registers a plant's response to music."

Abiotic stresses, notably extremes in temperature, photon irradiance, and supplies of water and inorganic solutes, frequently limit growth and productivity of major crop species such as wheat (*Triticum aestivum;* http://www.cimmyt.org/Research/Wheat/map/research_results/wphysio/wphysio.html). In addition, more than one abiotic stress can occur at one time. For example, high temperature and high photon irradiance often accompany low water supply, which can in turn be exacerbated by subsoil mineral toxicities that contain root growth. Furthermore, one abiotic stress can decrease a plant's ability to resist a second stress. Ultraviolet-B (UV-B) radiation can have a negative impact on the growth and development of plants.

For plants to respond to stimuli, activities of plant cells and structures have to be coordinated. Almost all plant communication is done by **hormones**. Hormones are low concentration chemical messengers active in another part of an organism. A response to stimuli is influenced by several hormones that are required in specific ratio. Hormones in turn require initiators which are plant growth regulators which are also naturally-occurring plant growth hormones.

Indoleacetic acid (IAA) is the most naturally occurring auxin. It is produced in shoot apical meristem, and found in young leaves, flowers and fruits. In a plant exposed to unidirectional light, auxin moves from bright side to shady side of a stem. Auxin binds to receptors and activates the ATP-driven proton pump. As hydrogen ions are pumped out of cells, cell wall becomes acidic, breaking hydrogen bonds. Cellulose fibrils, which are structural component of plant cell wall, are weakened and activated enzymes (activated by IAA within the cells) further degrade the cell wall. Electrochemical gradient established within the cell wall and its exterior environment causes uptake of solutes, similarly water enters the cells by osmosis. As a result turgid cell presses against cell wall, stretching it so that elongation occurs.

Gibberellins, a group of 70 plant hormones that differ chemically, are growth promoters that elongate cells. GA3 is the most naturally occurring gibberellins. Hormone GA3 binds to a receptor, a second messenger (Ca2+) inside cell which in turn combines with the protein **calmodulin**. Ca2+-calmodulin complex activates a gene coding for the enzyme amylase. Amylase acts on starch to release sugars used as a source of energy by growing cells.

Cytokinins are a class of plant hormones that promotes cell division. Cytokinins are derivatives of the purine base adenine. A natural cytokinin, zeatin, is found on corn kernels.

There are also found some inhibitory hormones that act on plants. Of them **Abscisic acid** and **ethylene** are most significant. Abscisic acid (ABA) is called "**stress hormone**." It maintains seed and bud dormancy and causes closure of stomata. ABA moves from leaves to vegetative buds in fall. Thereafter these buds are converted to winter buds which are covered by thick and hardened scales, an adaptation to counter cols stress. ABA brings about closing of stomata when its plant is under water stress. By some unknown mechanism, ABA causes K+ ions to leave guard cells. As a result guard cells lose water and stomata, thus preventing water loss.

It was an early practice to prepare citrus for market by storage in a room with kerosene stove. Later work revealed incomplete combustion of kerosene produced ethylene which ripens fruits! Ethylene is a gaseous plant hormone. It ripens fruits by increasing activity of enzymes that softens fruit.

Ethylene stimulates the production of cellulose enzyme that hydrolyzes cellulose in plant cell walls. A barrel of ripening apples can induce ripening of a bunch of bananas some distance away. Ethylene releasing from the site of a physical wound therefore can rotten a whole bunch of apple if one among them is wounded! The presence of ethylene in air generally inhibits growth of plants. Ethylene is involved in abscission (dropping) of leaves, fruits and flowers. Once abscission begins, ethylene stimulates production of enzymes such as cellulose that causes leaf, fruit or flower to drop.

So, from the above discussion we can come to the conclusion that plants also respond to external stimuli through growth (elongation, division or abscission) patterns. And hormones are the prime modulators of such manifestations.

References

Braam, J., and R.W. Davis, 1990, *"Rain-induced, Wind-induced, and Touch-induced Expression of Calmodulin and Calmodulin-related Genes,"* in *Arabidopsits Cell* 60: 357-67. (Talking Heads music at 60 db for 1 minute did not induce expression of touch-sensitive genes.)

Daedalus, 1991, "Green Music," *Nature* 351: 104 (explains fancifully how music might be used as an herbicide, claims Charles Darwin played the bassoon for *Mimosa pudica*).

Davis, R. and P. Scott, 2000, "Groovy plants; the influence of music on germinating seedlings and seedling growth," *J. Exp. Bot.* 51:73, (Sketchy abstract only that concludes that music does make seedlings grow faster, but the response is quite species-specific).

Isabelle, S. Booij-James, Shyam K. Dube, Marcel A.K. Jansen, Marvin Edelman and Autar K. Mattoo, *Plant Physiol*, Nov. 2000, vol. 124, pp. 1275-84. (Ultraviolet-B Radiation Impacts Light-Mediated Turnover of the Photosystem II Reaction Center Heterodimer in Arabidopsis Mutants Altered in Phenolic Metabolism.)

"Plants Alive with the Sound of Music", Researchers believe that plants thrive on melodious music, and shrivel and die with music that amounts to noise," *Deccan Herald*, 22nd May, 2005.

Subramanian, S., et al., 1969, "A Study on the Effect of Music on the Growth and Yield of Paddy," *Madras Agr*. J. 56: 510-16 (paddy is indifferent to daily 30-minute exposures to recorded south Indian oboe music).

Talos, 2001, "If Only Corn Had Ears," *ASPB News* 28 (6): 8-9. This brief article collected some references about sound and plants. I show here the references given in that article with Talos' original annotations.

Weinberger, P. and M. Measures, 1979, "Effects of the Intensity of Audible Sound on the Growth and Development of Dideau Winter Wheat," *Can. J. Bot.* 57: 1036-39. (A variety of sounds at 90 db had little effect, but plants subjected to 105-120 db showed reduced growth.)

17

Bioinformatics of Perception

S.N. Ojha

TOWARDS the end of the twentieth century, there were 24 complete genomes available in public databases,[1] including 16 bacterial, 6 archaeal, and 2 eukaryotic (*Saccharomyces cerevisiae and Caenorhabditis elegans*) genomes. In addition there have been an estimated 82 prokaryotic and 24 eukaryotic genome-sequencing efforts under way, including that of the human genome. Already fragments of most human genes and considerable fractions of the human and many other partially completed genomic sequences have been available in expressed-sequencetag (EST) data sets. Overall, nearly 5 billion nucleotides of sequence have been available in the GenBank database (release 115.0). At the same time it was also noted that "genome sequencing risks becoming expensive molecular stamp-collecting without the tools to mine the data and fuel hypothesis-driven laboratory-based research."[2] Such tools have since been emerging from the nascent science of bioinformatics, an interdisciplinary field that combines molecular biology with computer science, software engineering as well as some statistics. As this review illustrates through discussion on certain aspects of sensory biology, the bioinformatics is crucial to transforming the torrent of raw data into biological knowledge. Towards the closing of year 2004, there were 227 complete genome.[3]

The advent of whole-genome data resources — not only sequence but also other genome-scale data collections such as gene expression, protein interaction, and genetic variation — is causing two distinct yet complementary effects on the relatively new discipline of bioinformatics. First, the veritable flood of data is creating a need and demand for new tools for dealing adequately with the deluge, and second, the unprecedented extent, diversity, and impending completeness of the data sets are creating opportunities for new approaches to discovery based on computational methods.[4] In early 2001, a first draft of the human genome sequence was reported by Celera Genomics[5] and the International Human Genome Project Consortium.[6] Two groups have exploited this wealth of information publicly available from the latter project and have each produced a first draft of the human OR repertoire. [7, 8]. The diversity of odor recognition is mediated by odorant receptor (OR) genes. The overall conclusions are in accord with the information accumulated in the pre-genomic phase: There are ~ 1000 OR sequences in the human genome; the coding regions are intronless, the genes are spread over dozens of clusters, and more than half of OR sequences are pseudogenes. A major new finding is that chromosome 11 contains nearly half of the OR repertoire,[7, 8, 9] including a single cluster of ~ 100 OR Class I sequences. Similarly, the identification of "disease genes" and the mutations within them has greatly enhanced our understanding of normal function in the eye and ear.[10] With regard to human taste genetics, several recent discoveries demonstrate the power of human genetic approaches, but many interesting and important questions have not yet been answered. [11] The identification of "disease genes" and the mutations within them has greatly enhanced our understanding of normal function in the eye and ear. At the same time, it has become clear that these single-gene mutations must reside in a permissive genetic background for a disease phenotype to manifest. Segregating background genes can also modify the age of onset, rate of progression or severity of these diseases. These background genes that interact with the disease mutation and that are responsible for the specific phenotypes observed are commonly called genetic modifiers. Identification of these modifier genes may define the biological pathways that lead from the primary genetic defect to the aberrant phenotype.

Because all biological data are in some way information about how biology as a whole is organized, it is most valuable when systematically organized and integrated. Having these large collections of raw data, which include protein and RNA as well as genome sequences and structures, protein and RNA expression patterns, and cellular localization images, has created a huge need for databases to store information, provide access, and add value. For a current snapshot of the huge range of biological databases a good source is the annual special database issue of *Nucleic Acids Research,* published each January. It lists 339 databases in its opening review article in 2002.[12] Long before the first complete genome sequences of free living cells were determined, groups from around the world had been tackling the issues of (a) building repositories for raw data, (b) adding annotation to this raw data, and (c) providing higher level structure and organization. Examples of repositories are the public DNA sequence databases of EMBL, GenBank, and DDBJ as well as the public protein structure database PDB. Examples of annotation databases are Flybase, which maintained annotation around the genetics of *Drosphila* long before a genome sequence was available, and Swiss Prot, which adds functional annotation to protein sequences largely originating from mRNA and genomic sequencing. [13] Examples of organizational databases are Pfam, which groups protein sequence domains into families, thereby showing evolutionary relationships between paralogous proteins within an organism and orthologous proteins between organisms, SCOP, which groups more distantly related proteins together by structural similarity, and KEGG, which organizes proteins and ligands into networks of enzymic processes and regulatory networks.

These examples are only illustrative, as the roles are not even clear-cut in these cases, e.g. the DNA sequence repositories and organizational databases both contain some annotation. What differentiates the above databases from genome-sequence-based databases is that the former are all founded around primary sets of data that are currently unbounded, whereas in the case of the latter the primary dataset is essentially bounded. Though we do not know how many protein folds there are, we do know the complete DNA sequence for many organisms. One of the results of the integration of these existing databases with genome-sequence databases is that we can propagate this completeness to identify where the gaps in our knowledge lie.[14]

Facilities for storing, updating, accessing, querying, and otherwise manipulating the very data itself lie at the heart of the genomics enterprise. Aspects of the technology that are relevant to the sensory genomics are described here, along with the more important public databases and the pervasive character of the Internet and World Wide Web. The management of genomic information requires the long-term storage of its data and easy programmatic ways to access and update this information. Nearly all genome systems now use a relational database management system (RDBMS) as their core data store. The advantages of using RDBMS are as follows: (a) Considerable work in the theory and implementation has been undertaken in the computer science industry over the past two decades, providing well-understood, robust systems, in particular, with respect to back-ups and data integrity. (b) Relational databases use a structured query language (SQL), and all major programming languages have bindings to SQL interfaces, thus facilitating programmatic access. (c) There is a large pool of RDBMS and SQL-savvy programmers who can easily be brought into an RDBMS-based project. The main implementations are produced by Oracle or Sybase (which are commercial products) or Postgres or MySQL (which are open-source projects.) MySQL is not strictly an RDBMS, but for practical purposes it can be considered one and is widely used for genome data storage. For most systems direct programmatic access to the database is not encouraged, but instead a number of software abstractions are provided on top of the database. These abstractions, called an application programming interface (API) or a middleware layer, which allow the database schema to be insulated somewhat from the main set of programmatic clients to the system. These middleware layers differ in complexity and layout, but a number of systems, in particular Ensembl, Gadfly, Wormbase,[15] and Genquire, reuse the open-source projects Bioperl and BioJava[16] to provide a core set of interfaces. This reuse of interfaces sometimes provides the ability to mix and match components diretly (e.g. it is possible to use parts of the Genquire viewer with Ensembl directly), but more practically it eases the pain in porting components between projects. The genome management system must allow viewing and, for manual system, editing of the genomic annotation by users. For most of the previous decade the main system to use was the FMAP display of Acedb, which is still used in Wormbase and at all Sanger Institute for genome annotation. However the late 1990s saw the rise of the Web as the principle mode of communicating with the users, and the paradigm of "web views" of a database has been enthusiastically taken up by genome databases.

However, general-purpose relational databases, with their standardization and versatile query capability, now form the backbone of most large-scale sequence databases. At the same time, there is a trend towards object-oriented databases in the field, which actually underlie ACEDB and are now being used to create new specialized databases,[17] to back-fit existing databases,[18] to overlay relational databases,[19] etc. The advantages of object-oriented databases, in easier and richer modelling of complex domains such as molecular biology, are somewhat offset by the lack of standardization, especially in query tools. However, these concerns are being addressed, and efforts are also being made towards the use of common ontologies or comprehensive models of the domain,[20, 21] which may be necessary in the future to maintain consistency not only in object models but also in relational schemas.

Public Databases

The large number of databases, their degree of overlap, the rapid pace of change in the field, and funding issues have combined to produce a number of recent changes in the information environment,[22] including the end of some databases, such as the Genome Database at Johns Hopkins University, Baltimore, MD [subsequently resurrected at the Hospital for Sick Children in Toronto, Canada (http://www.gdb.org)] and the commercialization of others, such as SWISS-PROT.

The most useful axis on which to classify the databases remains the fundamental distinction between those housing primary data on the one hand and highly refined compilations on the other. The former are typified by the triad of coordinated nucleotide sequence databases, including GenBank, the DNA Databank of Japan, and the European Molecular Biology Laboratory, which depend on direct submissions from individual researchers, genome sequencing projects, and other sources and which monitor submissions but do little else in the way of refinement.[23] A recent trend, however, has been the increasing number of useful views on the data and comprehensive scope offered by institutions such as the NCBI, which is beginning to extend also to more active value-addition, as in the RefSeq collection (http://www.ncbi.nlm.nih.gov/LocusLink/refseq.html). Nevertheless, the consistency and quality of the author-provided annotation in the databases remain serious concerns that are just beginning to be addressed through technical approaches.[24] On the other extreme, SWISS-PROT, the highly curated database of protein sequences, remains a high-value resources available to the bioinformatics community, with its extensive annotation as to function, domain structure, post-translational modification, variants, etc. (http://www.expasy.ch/sprot or http://www. ebi.ac.uuk/sprot). Although it is continually being improved,[25] perhaps the most significant recent development in SWISS-PROT is a change in its funding status, by which it is now licensed to commercial users for a fee through a corporate entity (http://www.genebio.com) but remains free to academics. This typifies a new trend for highly curated databases in the field, one that is necessary to support the considerable manual effort associated with each of the increasing number of entries.

Web Resources

Beyond a doubt the most significant new trend has been the proliferation of highly specialized Web resources. The history of such enterprises generally follows one of three courses. In the first instance, it may remain a dedicated resource of limited appeal, maintained by the originator and perhaps a circle of like-minded colleagues. A second variety are those which may fall into disuse, and there are many such instances of moribund Websites that have not been updated for months or years, while "dead links" are increasingly a nuisance to Web navigation. Finally, a database that becomes unusually popular due to its coverage, features, or timeliness may, as a result, receive significant funding for maintenance and growth. Such resources may be associated with a particular algorithm or classification system for a broad swath of data, or they may support a sizeable research community, in particular those surrounding model organisms. In some cases such databases are so successful as to be commercialized in whole or in part, as was the Yeast Proteome Database.[26] Examples of Web resources abound, so much so that it would be fruitless to attempt a comprehensive review, particularly in light of their volatility. A sampling suffices to give the flavour. One can find many resources for particular gene families, a typical case being the G-protein-coupled receptors (GPCRs), extensively catalogued in both GCRDb [http://www.gcrdb.uthscsa.edu[27]] and GPCRDB [http://www./gcrdb.uthscsa.edu[28]]. A separate database, "GRAP." (http://www.grap.fagmed.uit no/GRAP/homepage.html), houses GPCR mutants,[29] whereas the subset of olfactory GPCRs is treated in the olfactory receptor database [ORDB, http://www.ycmi.med.yale.edu/senselab/ordb[30]]. These databases exhibit typical characteristics of the genre. What appear to be competing databases will often cross-reference each other, and most link to "standard" databases for sequence data, citations, etc.

To address the wealth of data described above, the computational biologists' toolbox continues to grow briskly, with wide-ranging theoretical and practical advances in recent years. The venerable BLAST software, long since the *sine qua non* of sequence database searching because of its efficient word-based algorithm and well-founded statistics, has been enhanced for genome-scale investigations in several ways. A new search engine, BLAST 2.0, provides increased speed and sensitivity, as well as support for several new variants of the basic algorithm, Gapped BLAST and position-specific, iterated (PSI)-BLAST. Gapped BLAST, as the name implies, allows for insertions and deletions within alignments, easing biological interpretation over longer regions. This capability is also provided by WU-BLAST2. PSI-BLAST combines two pre-existing techniques to provide a considerably more sensitive search. First, it melds an alignment of hits from an initial run of Gapped BLAST into a profile or position-specific scoring matrix, and then PSI-BLAST uses this profile to perform another search to draw more distant sequences into the alignment. This process is repeated until no further sequences are added to the set, resulting in a "family" of related sequences and a profile descriptor for that family. Dynamic programming is a well-known technique in computer science whereby tabular methods are used to store intermediate results and obviate their re-computation. As a rule, dynamic programming produces guaranteed optimal solutions for certain otherwise combinatorial problems but may be too expensive in time and space for large inputs, leading to the search for ways to speed the process and heuristics that sacrifice as litttle as possible of the sensitivity or other advantages of the "full" dynamic programming solution. The archetypal example in bioinformatics is the classic Smith-Waterman algorithm, which performs full optimal local alignment of sequences by dynamic programming[31] but which is generally too slow (without specialized hardware) for large-scale database searching, compared with BLAST. Perhaps the most widely used such collection is the Pfam database and its associated tools.[32] Pfam's protein domain families are based on Hidden Markov Model (HMM) representations, a kind of profile that makes use of a more sophisticated and versatile probabilistic model.[33] Recent developments in Pfam include the provision of an advanced version of the associated search software (HMMER), which is more sensitive and provides expectation values, and more complete database coverage, such that over 54 per cent of the proteins in SWISS-PROT and TREMBL now match one of the 1313 families in this database (release 3.1). HMMs, indeed, have proven to be very versatile computational constructs in the bioinformatics domain, and they are representative of a marked trend in the field in recent years toward Bayesian statistical methods.[34] The model-based approach to *ab initio* gene finding has culminated with the application of HMMs, which, because of their state-based architecture, are well suited to representing both cyclic transitions between exons and introns and the statistical and periodic properties within each such state, as well as boundary states and the profiles characteristic of biological signals. Moreover, HMMs have associated with the well-known dynamic programming algorithms not only for recognition of patterns but also for learning those patterns, within a well-founded Bayesian framework. These advantages have led to proliferation of HMM-based gene finders, including Genie, HMM-gene, and GeneMark.hmm. Other current trends in gene finding include several efforts with improved discriminant analysis techniques, including the FGENE family[35] and MZEF.[36]

Gene-Prediction Methods

Gene-prediction methods have traditionally been described as falling into two distinct approaches.[14] The first approach has been to use the statistical information contained within the genomic sequence to predict gene structures. The information used commonly includes compositional analysis of exons, introns, and splice sites, which may vary according to the background composition of the full genomic sequence. There are many programmes that perform this *ab initio* prediction, including Genscan, Fgenesh, HMMGene,[37] Grail, [38] and Genie. The algorithms behind these programmes are Hidden Markov Models (HMMs), neural networks, and Linear discriminant functions, although the majority now use HMMs. Genscan is commonly regarded to be the most accurate for predicting genes in the human genome, but all *ab initio* methods have a common weakness for large genomes. This weakness is partly due to the nature of genes in large vertebrate genomes. The amount of coding sequence compared to non-coding sequence is very small (approximately 2 per cent of the human genome is estimated to be coding), which leads to large introns and large intergenic regions with relatively small exons. For instance, the mean size of an exon in the human genome is 120 base pairs with the median intron size being ~ 2000 base pairs. The large non-coding regions lead the *ab initio* programmes astray and lead to extra genes being predicted in intergenic regions. The large introns within genes can also lead to extra exons being predicted within a true gene. The second approach to gene prediction has used the wealth of sequence data from genes that is already stored in the public sequence databases (SWISS-PROT, EMBL, RefSeq). These are commonly referred to as similarity-based approaches and are founded taking a protein or a cDNA and aligning it to the genomic sequence. There are many programmes that will do a local or global alignment of two sequences (BLAST), but for gene annotation these programmes are not good enough as they do not have any knowledge of gene structure: how to model splice sites, for instance. For accurate alignment of proteins or cDNAs to genomic sequences, programmes should be able to model splice sites, exons, introns, and in the case of protein alignment programmes, open reading frames. For aligning cDNAs to genomic sequences, programmes such as SIM4, EST GENOME, BLAST, and Exonerate are commonly used. Genewise and Procrustes are used for aligning proteins.

An Enormous Gene Family

The ability to detect smells serves essential and aesthetic functions in vertebrates.[39] Many species rely heavily on their sense of smell to locate food, detect predators or other dangers, navigate, and communicate societal information. Olfaction plays a role in mate choice, mother-infant recognition and signalling between members of a group.[40, 41] Humans may not depend on olfaction for survival to the same extent as other species, but we nevertheless use olfaction extensively to gather information on our sorroundings, from the student checking if her milk is still safe to drink, to the hunter using smell to help locate his prey, to the wine taster enjoying a vintage Bordeaux. Humans also communicate via odorants and pheromones, both consciously (by applying artificial scents) and subconsciously. For example, olfaction mediates the curious synchronization of menstrual cycles of women living in close proximity.[42] Aesthetically, olfaction is important for our enjoyment of food, our natural environment and our lives in general.[43] Human olfactory abilities are not well characterized, but it has been estimated that we can detect, although perhaps not discriminate, thousands of different odorants.

How do the nose and brain detect such a large array of small volatile chemicals and process that information into the perception of a smell? Multiple odorant molecules, differing in shape and chemical properties, must be discriminated.[39] This task is analogous to the recognition of diverse antigenes by the immune system. Both the olfactory and immune systems accomplish molecular recognition and discrimination by expressing many different receptors in the responding tissue. In olfaction, as many as 1000 different types of receptors are collectively used to detect thousands of different odorant molecules. Each receptor type is expressed in a subset of neurons in the olfactory epithelium, from which neurons wire directly to the olfactory bulb in the brain (reviewed in 30). From here, signals are relayed to the olfactory cortex,[44] where they result in the perception of smell. The astute prediction that odorant receptors would comprise a large family of seven-transmembrane-domain G-protein coupled receptors (GPCRs) expressed exclusively in the olfactory epithelium led to the cloning in 1991 of the first few olfactory receptor (OR) genes in rat.[45] This finding opened the way for characterization of the OR gene family, which was predicted on the basis of genomic library screens to comprise 1000 members in mammals.[46] Recently, exhaustive searches of the almost complete genome sequences of human and mouse have led to the identification of 906 human OR genes[7] and 1393[47] or 1296[48] mouse OR genes. These numbers extrapolate to a total of 950 human and 1500 mouse genes after missing sequences are accounted for.[7, 47] ORs are thus one of the largest known gene families in the human and mouse genomes, representing 3-5 per cent of all genes.[6] Several databases and websites have been developed to facilitate the study of these genes. It remains to be shown that each of these genes functions as an odorant receptor — most are denoted as such merely on the basis of sequence similarity to known ORs. Evidence of expression in the olfactory epithelium is available for only a limited number of mouse genes[49] and a handful of human genes.[50] Even fewer OR genes have been functionally expressed in heterologous cell types to confirm that they respond to odorants and elicit a signalling cascade.[51] Expression has been reported in non-olfactory tissues, principally the testis,[52] but also taste tissues,[53] prostate,[50] primordial germ cells,[54] erythroid cells,[55] heart[56] and notochord.[57] It is not clear whether the ectopic expression of these genes has functional significance,[58] perhaps as spermatid chemoreceptors in chemotaxis towards the egg,[52] or even as a developmental addressing system.[59] It is also possible that the transcripts observed in non-olfactory tissues are merely genomic contaminants in cDNA libraries and/or low-level illegitimate transcripts. Olfactory receptor gene sequences have also been reported from many other vertebrate species, including such phylogenetically diverse species as non-human primates,[60] pig,[61] dog,[27] rat,[45] dolphin,[62] marmot,[63] chicken,[64, 65] frog,[66] coelacanth,[62] catfish,[67] zebra fish,[68] mudpuppy,[69] lamprey,[70] medaka,[71] and goldfish.[72] Fish are estimated to have much smaller OR repertoires than mammals, with around 100 genes.[67] More distantly related chemosensory receptor genes have been described in fruit flies and nematode worms. Although all are 7-transmembrane domain GPCRs, the fly, worm, and vertebrate families appear to have arisen independently. Other mammalian families of more distantly related GPCRs, such as taste receptors (reviewed in 70) and pheromone receptors (reviewed in 4), are also involved in recognition of external chemical signals; these families also appear to have evolved independently of the OR family.

A startlingly high fraction of the human OR repertoire (at least 63 per cent) has degenerated to become pseudogenes, leaving only about 350 apparently functional OR genes.[7] In contrast, only about 20 per cent of mouse ORs are pseudogenes,[47] giving mice over three times as many intact genes as humans. Furthermore, some apparently intact human OR genes lack motifs that are very highly conserved in intact mouse OR genes, suggesting that not all human genes encode functional OR proteins.[47] These molecular differences may be the inevitable consequence of humans' reduced reliance on smell relative to rodents. However, it is not known whether their larger repertoire of functional genes enables mice to detect a wider range of odorants or to better distinguish closely related odorants than humans. When sequences are examined phylogenetically, intact human genes are found in most OR sub-families.[47] Thus, it is likely that humans can detect as wide a range of substances as mice, assuming that different OR subfamilies bind different odorant classes.

Taste Genetics

Humans show susbtantial differences in taste sensitivity to many different substances. Some of this variation is known to be genetic in origin, and many inter-individual differences are likely to be partially or wholly determined by genetic mechanisms. Recent advances in the understanding of taste at the molecular level have provided candidate genes that can be evaluated for contributions to phenotypic differences in taste abilities. Humans can distinguish five major taste classes: sweet, sour, bitter, salty and umami, a savory flavour exemplified by the amino acid glutamate.[73, 74, 75] Decades of careful work by sensory physiologists show that salty and sour perceptions are mediated by ion channels, whereas sweet, bitter and umami tastes are mediated by G-protein coupled receptors (GPCRs), all of which are expressed in taste cells within taste buds on the tongue.[76, 77]

Initial work in rodents demonstrated the existence of a group of genes that encode two main classes of taste GPCRs, the TAS1R family and the TAS2R family. Subsequent work extended these findings, with several important differences, to humans where these genes are designated TAS1R (or T1R) and TAS2R (or T2R), respectively.[78] There are 25 apparently functional TAS2R genes in humans, whose products are responsible for bitter perception.[79] The human TAS1R family contains just 3 genes, TAS1R1, TAS1R2, and TAS1R3, whose products form heterodimers that serve as either sweet receptors (TAS1R 2 + 3) or umami (TAS1R 1 + 3) receptors.[80] These GPCRs couple to specific intracellular G proteins. G α gustducin participates in bitter and sweet taste transduction,[81] and G γ 13 is involved in bitter perception.[82] Additional G proteins are also involved in these processes, but many specifics of this are currently unclear, such as what other G proteins are involved or whether different receptors couple to different G proteins. The receptors for salty and sour tastes are less well understood. Salt perception may be mediated by one of several ion channels. Evidence originally supported an amiloride-sensitive sodium channel as the mediator of salty taste,[83] although evidence for the involvement of another as yet undetermined channel in this process has emerged.[84] Sour taste is mediated by an acid sensor that, despite numerous proposed cellular mechanisms is still of uncertain molecular composition.[85]

The molecular sensors for all five taste classes act through second messenger systems to initiate neural signalling. These second messenger systems include phospholipase C –, cyclic AMP –, and IP3 – responsive mechanisms, although the precise second messenger mechanisms employed in many instances are not fully understood.[86] In many cases the second messenger systems cause release of calcium from intracellular stores,[87] leading to initiation of cell depolarization and transmission of neural impulses to the brain via the chroda tympani and glosspharyngeal nerves.[88]

The substantial majority of taste sensation in humans seems to be accounted for by the five main taste modalities described above. However, other taste modalities have been suggested. One of these is the taste of fats, which are an important source of calories in modern and pre-modern human diets. A specific taste of fat has not been demonstrated, although fats clearly impart a sensation ("mouth feel") that is desirable to humans. It may be significant that cells of the tongue produce a unique lipase, called lingual lipase. The protein encoded by this highly expressed gene may produce one or more lipid breakdown products that are recognized by a specialized chemosensory mechanism of unknown composition. Another possible taste is that of water.[74] Although water may have an effect on the taste sensory apparatus in other organisms, human subjects typically describe pure water as tasteless, and no strong psychophysical evidence exists that would assign a separate taste modality to water.

The field of human taste genetics is at an exciting juncture. Several recent discoveries demonstrate the power of human genetic approaches, but many interesting and important questions have yet to be answered. First, keep in mind that we do not know how much of the variation in human taste abilities is genetic in origin. Age, sex, and exposure to different diets and foods are known to affect some taste abilities.[89, 90] Disentangling genetic from non-genetic factors will require twin studies, segregation analysis, and other methods. If unlike PTC taste ability, sensitivity to other tastants is specified by a number of different genes, or by many allelic variants of one gene, each with small effects, this task will not be simple and may require large subject populations to produce clear conclusions.

An important area of bitter taste research currently addresses the coding problem, that is, what ligands are recognized by each of the bitter taste receptors? As suggested,[11] this problem may be better rephrased as: What is the bitter tastant ligand for each of the > 110 different bitter receptor proteins encoded by human populations worldwide? This question needs to be answered by a combination of *in vivo* studies using psychophysical measurements of taste abilities and their association with TAS2R gene variants plus *in vitro* biochemical studies of receptor ligand interactions.

Another largely unexamined area is variation in genes encoding taste-specific second messenger systems and downstream signalling components. Although SNPs associated with a number of these genes have been reported (http://www.ncbi.nlm.nih.gov/projects/SNP/), it is not clear how much variation remains to be discovered, nor do we know what effects such variants might have on taste perception. Recent human genetic studies of taste perception were strongly driven by the identification of genes encoding receptors and second messenger components of taste transduction. However, many gaps still exists in our knowledge of cellular and molecular aspects of taste perception. This suggests that a more traditional approach, involving linkage and whole-genome association studies, might identify genes that are currently not known or suspected to be involved in our sense of taste.

Taste perception appears to play a large role in a number of different behaviours with important effects on human health, including alcohol consumption, nicotine usage, and food choices.[91, 92] Many of these behaviours, such as alcohol consumption, have a substantial genetic contribution.[93] It is possible that some of this genetic contribution is mediated at the level of inherited variation in taste preferences. Supporting this view is a recent finding that variation in TAS2R 38 (PTC) gene is strongly correlated with the perceived taste of alcohol, and remarkably, with alcohol consumption.[94] As efforts to better understand and modulate potentially harmful dietary choices gain importance, so will our need to understand the genetic underpinnings of individual differences in taste perception.

Gene Discovery in the Auditory System

An understanding of the complexities and beauty of the biological process of hearing itself is unfolding as genes underlying hereditary hearing impairment are identified.[95] Genes involved in modifying hearing are also being found, and will be critical to a full comprehension of genotype-phenotype relationships. It has long been recognized that heredity plays a major role in hearing impairment. Despite the fact that understanding the genetic basis of hearing loss has fascinated human and medical geneticists for decades, only within the past few years have the genes and molecular mechanisms underlying deafness begun to be discovered. In part, this results from various obstacles to investigation of the auditory system including: inaccessibility of the sensory end organ for hearing, the cochlea, within the dense temporal bone; length of time to direct pathologic observation of the deaf ear due to an otherwise normal lifespan of individuals with hearing loss; unparalleled genetic heterogeneity; and assortative mating.

The frequency of hearing loss is estimated at one per thousand newborns and half of all cases are attributed to genetic causes. In addition to being a common etiology of congenital deafness, mutations in genes are responsible for progressive hearing loss, and no doubt will be found to play an important role in progressive hearing loss with ageing (presbycusis). Hundreds of syndromic forms of deafness have been described[96, 97, 98] and the underlying genetic mutation identified for many of the more common forms, but only 30 per cent of genetic cases are estimated to be part of a heritable syndrome. Thus, the vast majority of genetic deafness is designated as non-syndromic and to date over 65 loci have been mapped. Non-syndromic hearing impairment is categorized further by mode of inheritance: approximately 77 per cent of cases are autosomal recessive; 22 per cent autosomal dominant; 1 per cent X-linked; and <1 per cent due to mitochondrial inheritance.[99] Dominant loci are designated with the prefix "DFNA," recessive loci "DFNB", X-linked loci "DFN" and modifying loci with "DFNM."

Generally, patients with autosomal recessive hearing impairment have prelingual and congenital deafness and patients with autosomal dominant hearing impairment have postlingual and progressive hearing impairment. This observation may be explained by the complete absence of functional protein in recessive disorders, while in autosomal dominant disorders, dominant mutations may be consistent with initial function and subsequent hearing impairment due to cumulative, degenerative process. A recent tally of non-syndromic hearing loss disorders reveals 32 autosomal dominant, 27 autosomal recessive, and 4 X-linked forms.[98] It remains to be shown whether each of these loci will correspond to a unique gene.

Inspection of the genes identified in hearing disorders and those among the gene lists from the EST sequencing projects reveals a great diversity of transcripts, perhaps not surprising due to the large variety of cells and complexity of the inner ear. The finding of a large percentage of cochlear ESTs not identified in any other tissue may indicate the existence of genes that are unique to the cochlear. Certainly, the great degree of genetic heterogeneity reflected in the many different syndromes involving hearing loss and mapped loci is indicative of a large number of genes orchestrating the hearing process. Grouping the genes discovered to be etiologic in deafness disorders into functional categories begins the process of understanding their role in hearing. Knowledge of the pathways in which many of these genes function will be an exciting journey in hearing science; no doubt pathways exist that are not yet imagined. Another important aspect of gene discovery for deafness disorders is that it makes possible the development of diagnostic tests and accurate genetic counselling.

Appropriate medical management and therapeutic options may be based on an understanding of the specific disorder.

Several preferentially expressed cochlear genes, namely COCH[100] and OTOR,[101, 102] have been identified from the human fetal cochlear cDNA library, COCH was further shown to be responsible for a sensorineural deafness and vestibular disorder, DFNA9.[103]

Another group of genes of intense interest are those required for survival of sensory hair cells. The POU domain transcription factor gene POU4F3 is required for terminal differentiation and maintenance of inner hair cells and an 8 bp deletion in the POU homeodomain results in progressive hearing loss in DFNA15.[104] Studies of such genes may result in valuable insight into the molecular triggers for hair cell degeneration. Loss of hair cells is presumed to be a fundamental cause of progressive age-related hearing loss (presbycusis) and an understanding of this degenerative process might provide the basis for therapeautic intervention. The recent finding of the transmembrane cochlear-expressed gene TMC1 uncovers a common cause of non-syndromic recessive deafness in Pakistan and India at the DFNB7/B11 locus on chromosome 9 in bands q13-q21; mutations in TMC1 account for the deafness phenotype in 5.4 – 3.0 per cent of 230 families screened.[105]

Molecular analyses of the auditory system have already yielded a number of genes in mice and humans that influence the expression or function of other genes. Studies of these genes are certain to provide insight into the interaction of their gene products.

A variety of mitochondrial disorders have been found to involve hearing loss, perhaps reflecting the highly metabolic state of the hearing process.[60] Of particular interest has been the A 1555→ G mutation in 12S rRNA that is recognized as the most frequent cause of aminoglycoside-induced deafness and as the etiology of a non-syndromic deafness.[106] In a recent study a nearly identical degree of mitochondrial dysfunction was observed in enucleated lymphoblastoid cells derived from both symptomatic and asymptomatic individuals from the same kindred[107] supporting the possibility of a nuclear gene in modifying the effect of the mutation.

Investigations in hereditary deafness have revealed many lessons in genetics, foremost among them a sensory system with profound genotypic and phenotypic heterogeneity. Despite the recent tremendous successes in the genetics of deafness, our knowledge remains woefully incomplete. An astonishing number of deafness loci have been mapped in humans and mice, yet the genetic basis of many disorders remains unknown.

Genomic approaches using a combination of methods of positional cloning, candidate genes and mouse models continue to yield new and novel genes providing valuable insight into the molecular basis of the process of hearing.

Modifier Genes for Vision Impairment

Modifier genes can affect the phenotypic outcome of a given genotype by interacting in the same or a parallel biological pathway as a "disease gene." The effect can be enhancing, leading to a more severe mutant phenotype, or suppressive, reducing the mutant phenotype even to the extent of completely restoring the normal condition. Modifier genes can also alter the pleiotropy of a given disease, resulting in different combinations of traits. In addition, for any given disorder, multiple modifier genes may act in combination to create a final, cumulative effect on the expression of a phenotype.

The visual process involves a complex set of physiochemical reactions that convert light energy into neuronal signals that transmit information to the brain. The anterior part of the eye (including lens, cornea, pupil, iris and ciliary body) is responsible for maintaining optimal conditions for light to enter the eye. This involves providing a clear, well-nourished, surface with proper supporting tissue for the cornea and lens to refract the right amount of light onto the retina without any interference. The posterior portion of the eye (the retina and optic nerve) is required for the conversion of light energy into chemical and electrical stimuli and subsequent transmission of the sensory neural signals to the visual cortex of the brain. Absorption of light causes a structural change in chromophores in the photoreceptor cell that through a signalling cascade causes membrane hyperpolarization and changes in neurotransmitter release at the photoreceptor/bipolar cell synapse. The signal is then transmitted by neuronal cells (bipolar and ganglion cells) through the optic nerve to the visual cortex in the brain. Defects in any portion of the eye can disrupt the visual process, affecting visual acuity as well as discrimination of texture, depth and motion. Many of the genes involved in the visual cascade have been identified in recent years. At present, almost 300 genes are associated with ocular disease; over 200 of these genes cause retinal disorders that affect the visual cascade and retinal development, and approximately 50 genes are associated with anterior eye defects. (http://www3.ncbi.nlm.nih.gov/Omim/, http://www.sph.uth.tmc.edu/Retnet/disease.htm). Additional ocular diseases have been associated with particular chromosomal regions, but the underlying genes remain to be identified. (http://www.sph.uth.tme.edu./Retnet/disease.htm.,http://genetics.med.harvard.edu/_cepko/SAGE/).[47]

Phenotypic variation has been reported for many of the described ocular diseases, indicating the potential presence of genetic modifiers. An early, classic example suggesting modifier effects is the report of a nuclear family in which different members carrying the same deletion in their RDS gene develop retinitis pigmentosa (RP,) pattern dystrophy or fundus flavimaculatus.[108] Although the genes underlying the above modifications have yet to be identified, one gene that is known to interact with RDS is ROM1.

Three more recent publications involving the retinitis pigmentosa 1 (RP1), primary open-angle glaucoma (POAG) and Bardet-Biedl syndrome (BBS) genes also suggest genetic modifiers effects. In a recent study of 1941 probands with a clinical diagnosis of retinitis pigmentosa, 17 patients were shown to harbour mutations within their RP1 gene.[109] The most common mutation found was a premature stop codon, Arg-677Ter.

Evidence of phenotypic modifiers has also been reported in patients with POAG who have mutations within their myocilin (MYOC) gene. In a population study of 1730 probands, the most ferequent mutation, Gln368Ter, was associated with adultonset POAG and elevated intraocular pressure. Haplotype anlaysis among individuals with the Gln368Ter mutation suggested a founder effect or common ancestor. Despite this, patients with this particular mutation showed variation both in age of onset and in disease severity, which ranged from ocular hypertension to legal blindness with severe visual field loss.[110]

Finally, a recent report identifies mutations in more than one gene in individuals with BBS, a pleiotropic disorder with many clinical features, including pigmentary retinopathy. The disease is genetically heterogeneous and is inherited in an autosomal recessive manner, but variability in phenotypic expressivity of BBS is well documented.[111, 112] Several of the BBS genes have recently been identified.[113] It has been postulated that the genes at independent BBS loci could interact in a common pathway. One particular finding[114] notes the presence of homozygosity for a mutation at the BBS6 locus and simultaneously the presence of heterozygosity for another mutation at a second BBS locus. The authors term the inheritance "triallelic," suggesting a mode of disease transmission requiring mutations in genes at two independent loci in order for the disease to manifest. One way in which the data of the three mutant BBS alleles have been interpreted is that the disease in inherited in a recessive manner with one of the genes serving as a modifier of penetrance.[115] The third BBS allele identified in the report by Katsanis et al.[114] may represent such a gene, in accord with the definition of modifiers as genes at independent loci, that interact with the primary disease gene to alter the phenotype.

The degree to which a phenotype is altered by modifiers and the method by which the alteration occurs is uncharted territory. Discoveries like those described above are intriguing. Study of diseases such as BBS with complex inheritance patterns will greatly aid in elucidating the variety of gene-gene interactions that occur in occular diseases.

Notes

1. N.C. Kyrpides, 1999, Genomes Online Database (GOLD 1.0): A monitor of complete and ongoing genome projects worldwide. *Bioinformatics*, 15 (9), 773-74.
2. M.J. Pallen, 1999, "Microbial genomes," *Mol. Microbiol*, 32(5), 907-12.
3. J. Gough, 2005, *Convergent Evolution of Domain Architectures* (is rare). vol. 21, no. 8, 2005, 1464-71.
4. D.B. Searls, 2000, "Bioinformatics tools for whole genomes," *Annu. Rev. Genomics Hum. Genet*, 2000, 01, 251-79.
5. J.C. Venter, MD. Adams, E.W. Myres, P.W. Li, R.J. Mural, et. al. 2001, "The sequence of the human genome," *Science*, 291, 1304-51.
6. Int. Hum. Genome Seq. Consort, 2001, "Initial sequencing and analysis of the human genome," *Nature*, 409:8760-921.
7. G. Glusman, I. Yanai, I. Rubin and D. Lancet, 2001, "The complete human olfactory subgenome," *Genome*, Res., 11, 685-702.
8. S. Zozulya, F. Echeverri, T. Nguyen, 2001, "The human olfactory receptor repertorire," *Genome Biol.*, 2:0018, 1-12.
9. J.A. Buettner, G. Glusman, N. Ben-Arie, P. Ramos, D. Lancet,

G.A. Evans, 1998, "Organization and evolution of olfactory receptor genes on human chromosome 11," *Genomics,* 53:56-68.

10. N.B. Haider, A, lkeda, K. Jürgen, K. Naggert Jürgen and P.M. Nishina, 2002, "Genetic modifiers of vision and hearing," *Hum. Mol. Genet.,* vol. 11, no. 10, 1195-1206.

11. D. Drayna, 2005, "Human Taste Genetics," *Annu. Rev. Genomics Hum. Genet,* 6:217-35.

12. A.D. Baxevanis, 2002, "The Molecular Biology Database Collection: 2002 update," *Nucleic Acids Res.* 30:1-12.

13. A. Bairoch, R. Apweiler, 2000, "The SWISS-PROT protein sequence database and its supplement TrEMBL in 2000," *Nucleic Acids Res.* 28:45-48.

14. E. Birney, M. Clamp, and T. Hubbard, 2002, "Database and tools for browsing genomes," *Annu. Rev. Genomics Hum, Genet,* 2002, 3:293-310.

15. L. Stein, P. Sternberg, R. Durbin, J. Thierry-Mieg, J. Spieth, 2001, "WormBase: Network access to the genome and biology of Caenorhabditis elegans," *Nucleic Acids. Res.* 29, 82-86.

16. M.R. Pocock, T. Down, T.J.P. Hubbard, 2000, "BioJava: Open source components for bioinformatics," *SIGBIO Newsl,* 20, 10-12.

17. F.A. Kolpakov, E.A. Ananko, G.B. Kolesov, N.A. Kolchanov, 1998, "GeneNet: a gene network database and its automated visualization," *Bioinfomatics* 14(6): 529-37.

18. D. Ghosh, 1999, "Object oriented transcription factors database (OOTFD)," *Nucleic Acids Res.,* 27(1):315-17.

19. I.M. Chen, A.S. Kosky, V.M. Markowiz, E. Szeto, T. Topaloglou, 1998, "Advanced query mechanisms for biological databases," *Intell. Syst. Mol. Biol.* 6:43-51.

20. P.G. Baker, C.A. Goble, S. Bechhofer, N.W. Paton, R. Stevens, A. Brass, 1999, "An ontology for bioinformatics applications," *Bioinformatics* 15(6):510-20.

21. S. Schulze-Kremer, 1998, "Ontologies for molecular biology," *Pac. Symp. Biocomput,* 3, 695-706.

22. L.B. Ellis, and D. Kalumbi, 1999, "Financing a future for public biological data," *Bioinformatics* 15(9):717-22.

23. G. Stoesser, M.A. Tuli, R. Lopez, P. Sterk, 1999, "The EMBL Nucleotide Sequence Database," *Nucleic Acids. Res.* 27(1), 18-24.

24. F. Eisenhaber, P. Bork, 1999, "Evalution of human-readable

annotation in biomolecular sequence databases with biological rule libraries," *Bioinformatics* 15(7):528-35.

25. A. Bairoch, R. Apweiler, 1999, "The SWISS-PROT protein sequence data bank and its supplement TrEMBL in 1999," *Nucleic Acids Res.* 27(1): pp. 49-54.

26. P.E. Hodges, A.H. McKee, B.P. Davis, W.E. Payne, J.I. Garrels, 1999, "The Yeast Proteome Database (YPD): A model for the organization and presentation of genome-wide functional data," *Nucleic Acids Res.*, 27, 69-73.

27. L. Issel-Tarver and J. Rine, 1996, "Organization and expression of canine olfactory receptor genes," *Proc. Natl. Acad. Sci. USA*, 93, 10897-02.

28. F. Horn, J. Weare, M.W. Beukers, S. Hüorsch, A. Bairoch, et al., 1998, "GPCRDB: An information system for Gprotein-coupled receptors," *Nucleic Acids Res.* 26(1) 277-81.

29. K. Kristiansen, S.G. Dahl, Ø Edvardsen, 1996, "A database of mutants and effects of site-directed mutagenesis experiments on G-protein coupled receptors," *Proteins: Struct. Funct. Genet.* 26, 81-94.

30. E. Skoufos, M.D. Healy, M.S. Singer, P. M. Nadkarni, P.L. Miller, G.S. Shephred, 1999, "Olfactory Receptor database: A database of the largest eukaryotic gene family," *Nucleic Acids Res.* 1, 343-45.

31. T.F. Smith, M.S. Waterman, (1981), "Identification of Common Molecular Sequences," *J. Mol. Biol.* 147(1), 195-97.

32. A. Bateman, E. Birney, R. Durbin, S.R. Eddy, R.D. Finn, E.L. Sonnhammer, 1999, "Pfam 3.1: 1313 multiple alignments and profile HMMs match the majority of proteins," *Nucleic Acids Res.* 27(1):260-62.

33. S.R. Eddy, 1998, "Profile hidden Markov models," *Bioinformatics* 14(9):755-63.

34. R. Durbin, R. Eddy, A. Krogh, G. Mitchison, 1998, *Biological Sequence Analysis: Probabilistic Models of Proteins and Nucleic Acids,* New York: Cambridge Univ. Press.

35. V. Solovyev, A. Salamov, 1997, "The Gene-Finder computer tools for analysis of human and model organisms genome sequences," *Intell. Syst, Mol, Biol,* 5, 294-302.

36. M.Q. Zhang, 1997, "Identification of protein coding regions in the human genome by quadratic discriminant anlaysis," *Proc. Natl. Acad. Sci., USA*, 94(2), 565-68.

37. A. Krogh, 2000, "Using database matches with HMMGene for automated gene detection in Drosophila," *Genome Res.* 10: 523-28.

38. Y. Xu, E.C. Uberbacher, 1997, "Automated gene identification in large-scale genomic sequences," *J. Comput, Biol.* 4, 325-38.

39. J.M. Young and B.J. Trask, 2002, "The sense of smell: Genomics of vertebrate odorant receptors," *Hum. Mol. Genet.* vol. 121, no. 10, 1153-60.

40. D.M. Stoddart, 1980, *The Ecology of Vertebrate Olfaction,* London: Chapman and Hall.

41. D. Malakoff, 1999, "Following the scent of avian olfaction," *Science*, 286, 704-05.

42. K. Stern and M.K. McClintock, 1998, "Regulation of ovulation by human pheromones," *Nature*, 392, 177-79.

43. T. Miwa, M. Furukawa, T. Tsukatani, R.M. Costanzo, L.J. DiNardo and E.R. Reiter, 2001, "Impact of olfactory impairment on quality of life and disability," *Arch. Otolayngol. Head Neck Surg.*, 127, 497-503.

44. Z. Zou, L.F. Horowitz, J.P. Montmayeur, S. Snapper, and L.B. Buck, 2001, "Genetic tracing reveals a stereotyped sensory map in the olfactory cortex," *Nature*, 414, 173-79.

45. L. Buck and R. Axel, 1991, "A novel multigene family may encode odorant receptors: a molecular basis for odour recognition," *Cell*, 65, 175-87.

46. L.B. Buck, 1992, "The olfactory multigene family," *Curr. Opin. Genet Dev.*, 2, 467-73.

47. J.M. Young C. Friedman, E.M. Williams, J.A. Ross, L. Tonnes-Priddy and B.J. Trask, 2002, "Different evolutionary processes shaped the mouse and human olfactory receptor gene families," *Hum. Mol. Genet.* 11. 535-46.

48. X. Zhang, and S. direstein, 2002, "The olfactory receptor gene superfamily of the mouse," *Nat. Neurosci.*, 5, 124-33.

49. R.P. Laqne, T. Cutforth, J. Young, M. Athanasiou, C. Friedman, L. Rowen, G. Evans, R. Axel, L. Hood, B.J. trask, 2001, "Genomic analysis of orthologous mouse and human olfactory receptor loci" *Proc. Natl. Acad. Sci. USA*, 98, 7390-95.

50. T.T. Yuan, P. Toy, J.A. McClary, R.J. Lin, N.G. Miyamoto and P.J. Kretschmer, 2001, "Cloning and genetic characterization of an evolutionarily conserved human olfactory receptor that is differentially expressed across species," *Gene*. 278, 41-51.

51. H. Hatt, K. Lang and G. Gisselmann, 2001, "Functional expression and characterization of odorant receptors using the Semliki Forest Virus System," *Biol. Chem.*, 382, 1207-24.

52. M. Parmentier, F. Libert, S. Schurmans, S. Schiffmann, A. Lefort, D. Eggeri C. Ledent, C. Mollerau, C. Gerard, J. Perret, et al., 1992, "Expression of members of the putative olfactory receptor gene family in mammalian germ cells," *Nature*, 355, 453-55.

53. M.B. Thomas, S.L. Haines and R.A. Akeson, 1996, "Chemoreceptors expressed in taste, olfactory and male reproductive tissues," *Gene*, 178, 1-5.

54. T. Goto, A. Salpekar and M. Monk, 2001, "Expression of a testis-specific member of the olfactory receptor gene family in human primordial germ cells," *Mol. Hum. Reported.*, 7, 553-58.

55. E.A. Feingold, L.A. Penny, A.W. Nienhuis and B.G. Forget, 1999, "An olfactory receptor gene is located in the extended human beta-globin gene cluster and is expressed in erythroid cells," *Genomics*, 61, 15-23.

56. G. Drutel, J.M. Arrang, J. Diaz, C. Wisnewsky, K. Schwartz and J.C. Schtwartz, 1995, "Clonning of OL1, a putative olfactory receptor and its expression in the developing rat heart," *Receptors Channels*, 3, 33-40.

57. S. Nef and P. Nef, 1997, "Olfaction: Transient expression of a putative odorant receptor in the avian notochord," *Proc. Natl. Acad. Sci.*, USA, 94, 4766-71.

58. A. Branscomb, J. Seger and R.L. White, 2000, "Evolution of odorant receptors expressed in mammalian testes," *Genetics*, 156, 785-97.

59. W.J. Dreyer, 1998, "The area code hypothesis revisited: olfactory receptors and other related transmembrance receptors may function as the last digits in a cell surface code for assembling embroys," *Proc. Natl Acad. Sci. USA*, 95, 9072-77.

60. S. Rouquier, A. Blancher, and D. Giorgi, 2000, "The olfactory receptor gene repertoire in primates and mouse : Evidence for reduction of the functional fraction in primates," *Proc. Natl. Acad. Sci.*, USA, 97, 2870-74.

61. V. Matarazzo, A. Tirad, M. Renucci, A. Belaich and J.L. Clement, 1998, "Isolation of putative olfactory receptor sequences from pig nasal epitheliu7m," *Neurosci. Lett.*, 249, 87-90.

62. J. Freitag, G. Ludwig, I Andreini, P. Rossler and H. Breer, 1998, "Olfactory receptors in aquatic and terrestrial vertebrates," *J. Comp. Physiol.* [A], 183, 635-50.

63. V. Matarazzo, A. Tirard, M. Renucci, J.M. Botto, M.C. Bel, J.M. Claverie, A. Belaich and J.L. Clement, 2000, "Identification of odorant receptors from the Alpine marmot (Marmota marmota.)" *Cell. Mol. Biol.* (Noisy-le-grand,) 46, 1249-58.

64. S. Nef, I. Allaman, H. Fiumelli, E. De Castro and P. Nef, 1996, "Olfaction in birds: Differential embryonic expression of nine putative odorant receptor genes in the avian olfactory system," *Mech. Dev.*, 55, 65-77.

65. M. Leibovici, F. Lapointe, P. Aletta and C. Ayer-Le Lievre, 1996, "Avian olfactory receptors: Differentiation of olfactory neurons under normal and experimental conditions," *Dev. Biol.*, 175, 118-31.

66. J. Freitag, J. Krieger, J. Strotmann and H. Breer, 1995, "Two classes of olfactory receptors in Xenopus laevis," *Neuron*, 15, 1383-92.

67. J. Ngai, M.M. Dowling, L. Buck, R. Axel and A. Chess, 1993, "The family of genes encoding odorant receptors in the channel catfish," *Cell*, 72, 657-66.

68. J.C. Dugas and J. Ngai, 2001, Analysis and characterization of an ordorant receptor gene cluster in the zebrafish genome," *Genomics*, 71, 53-65.

69. Q. Zhou, G. Hinkle, M.L. Sogin and V.E. Dionne, 1997, "Phylogenetic analysis of olfactory receptor genes from mudpuppy (Necturus maculosus)," *Biol. Bull.*, 193, 248-50.

70. J. Frietag, A. Back, G. Ludwig, L. von Buchholtz and H. Breer, (1999), "On the origin of the olfactory receptor family: Receptor genes of the jawless fish, (Lampetra fluviatilils)," *Gene*, 226, 165-74.

71. R. Kondo, S. Kaneko, H. Sun, M. Sakaizumi and S.I. Chigusa, 2002, "Diversification of olfactory receptor genes in the Japanse medaka fish, Oryzias latipes," *Gene*, 282, 113-20.

72. Y. Cao, B.C. Oh, and L. Styer, 1998, "Cloning and localization of two multigene receptor families in goldfish olfactory epithelium," *Proc. Natl. Acad. Sci. USA*, 95, 11987-92.

73. S. Kinnamon, R. Margolskee, 1996, "Mechanisms of taste transduction," *Curr. Opin. Neurobiol*, 6, 506-13.

74. B. Lindemann, 1996, "Taste perception," *Physiol. Rev.* 76, 719-66.

75. B. Lindemann, Y. Ogiwara, Y. Ninomiya, 2002, "The Discovery of Umami," *Chem. Senses*, 27, 843-44.

76. T. Gilbertson, S. Damak, R. Margolskee, 2000, "The molecular physiology of taste transduction," *Curr, Opin, Neurobiol,* 10: 519-27.

77. D. Smith, R. Margolskee, 2001, "Making sense of taste," *Sci. Am.* 284, 32-39.

78. X. Li, L. Staszewski, H. Xu, K. Durick, M. Zoller, E. Adler, 2002, "Human receptors for sweet and umami taste," *Proc. Natl. Acad. Sci. USA,* 1999, 4692-96.

79. G. Wong, K. Gannon, R. Margolskee, 1996, "Transduction of bitter and sweet taste by gustducin," *Nature,* 381, 796-800.

80. L. Huang, Y. Shanker, J. Dbyauskaite, J. Zheng, W. Yan, et al., 1999, "Gg 13 colocalizes with gustducin in taste receptor cells and mediates IP3 responses to bitter denatonium," *Nat. Neurosci.* 2: 1055-62.

81. G. Heck, S. Mierson, J. DeSimone, 1984, "Salt taste transduction occurs thorugh an amiloride-sensitive sodium transport pathway," *Science* 223:403-5.

82. U.K. Kim, P. Breskin, D. Reed, D. Drayna, 2004. "Genetics of human taste perception," *J. Dental Res.* 83, 448-53.

83. C. Ossebaard, D. Smith, 1995, "Effect of amiloride on the taste of NaCl, Nagluconate and KCl in humans: Implications for Na+receptor mechanisms," *Chem. Senses* 20, 37-46.

84. B. Lindemann, 2001, "Receptors and transduction in taste," *Nature,* 413, 219-25.

85. B. Bufe, P. Breslin, C. Kuhn, C. Tharp, et al., 2005, "The molecular bases of individual differences in phyenythiocarbamide and propylthiouracil bitterness perception," *Curr. Biol.* 15:1-20.

86. U.K. Kim, E. Jorgenson, H. Coon, M. Leppert, N. Risch, D. Drayna, 2003, "Positional cloning of the human quantitative trait locus underlying taste sensitivity to phenylthiocarbamide," *Science,* 299, 1221-25.

87. G.Q. Zhao, Y. Zhang, M. Hoon, J. Chandrashekar, I. Erlenback, et al., 2003, "The receptors for mammalian sweet and umami taste," *Cell,* 115, 255-66.

88. G. Hellekant, B. Danilova, Y. Ninomiya, 1997, "Primate sense of taste: behavioral and single chroda tympani and glossopharyngealnerve fibre recordings in the rhesus monkey, Macca Mulatta," *J. Neurophysiol,* 77: 978-93.

89. L. Bartoshuk, V. Duffy, I. Miller, 1994, "PTC/PROP tasting: anatomy, psychophysics and sex effects," *Physiol, Behav*, 56:1165-71.

90. H. Kalmus, 1958, "Improvement in the classification of the taster genotypes," *Ann. Hum. genet*, 22, 222-30.

91. M. Enoch, C. Harris, D. Goldman, 2001, "Does a reduced sensitivity to bitter taste increase the risk of becoming nicotine addicted?," *Addict. Behav*. 26:399-404.

92. B. Tepper, 1998, "Genetics of perception '98, 6-n-propylthiouracyl: a genetic marker for taste, with implications for food preference and dietary habits," *Am. J. Hum. Genet*, 63, 1271-76.

93. J. Kaprio, M. Koskenvuo, H. Langivainio, K. Romanov, S. Sarna, R. Rose, 1987, "Genetic influences on use and abuse of alochol: A study of 5638 adults by Finnish twin brothers," *Alcohol. Clin. Exp. res*. 11, 349-56.

94. V. Duffy, A. Davidson, J. Kidd, K. Kidd, W. Speed, et al., 2004, "Bitter receptor gene (TAS2R38,) 6-n-propylthiouracil (PROP) bitterness and alchol intake," *Alcohol. Clin. Exp. Res*. 28(11):1629-37.

95. Cynthia C. Morton, 2002, "Genetics, genomics and gene discovery in the auditory system," *Hum. Mol. Genet*., 2002, vol. 11, No. 10, 1229-40.

96. R. J. Gorlin, H.V. Toriello and M.M., 1995, *Hereditary Hearing Loss and its Syndromes*, New York: Oxford University Press.

97. OMIM, Online Mendelian Inheritance in Man: www.ncbi.nlm.nih.gov/entrez/query.fcgi?db=OMIM.

98. Camp G. Van, and R.J.H. Smith, *Hereditary hearing loss homepage*.

99. N.E. Morton, "Genetic epidemiology of hearing impairment," *Ann. N.Y. Acad, Sci*. 630, 16-31.

100. N.G. Robertson, A.B. Skvorak, Y. Yin, S. Weremowicz, K.R. Johnson, K.A. Kovatch, J.F. Battey, F.R. Bieber and C.C. Morton, 1997, "Mapping and characterization of a novel cochlear gene in human and in mouse: a positional candidate gene for A deafness disorder, DFNA9," *Genomics*, 46, 345-54.

101. N.G. Robertson, S. Heller, J.S. Lin, B.L. Resendes, S. Weremowicz, C.S. Denis, A.M. Bell, A.J. Hudspeth and C.C. Morton, 2000, "A novel conserved cochlear gene, OTOR: Identification, expression analysis and chromosomal mapping," *Genomics*, 66, 242-48.

102. N.D. Rendtorff, M. Frodin, T. Attie-Bitach, M. Vekemans and N. Tommerup, 2001, "Identification and characterization of an inner ear-expressed human melanoma inhibitory activity (MIA)-like gene (MIAL) with a frequent polymorphism that abolishes translation," *Genomics*, 71, 40-52.

103. N.G. Robertson, L. Lu., S. Heller, S.N. Merchant, R.D. Eavey, M. McKenna, J.B. Nadol, Jr., R..T. Miyamoto, F.H. Linthicum, Jr., J.F. Lubianca Neto, et al. 1998, "Mutations in a novel cochlear gene cause DENA 9, a human non-sydromic deafness with vestibular dysfunction," *Nat. Genet*, 20, 299-303.

104. O. Vahava, R. Morell, E.D. Lynch, S. Weiss, M.E. Kagan, N. Ahituv, J.E. Morrow, M.K. Lee, A.B. Skvorak, C.C. Morton, et al., 1998, "Mutation in transcription factor POU4F3 associated with in herited progressive hearing loss in humans," *Science*, 279, 1950-54..

105. K. Kurima, L.M. Peters, Y. Yang, S. Riazuddin, Z.M. Ahmed, S. Naz, D. Arnaud, S. Drury, J. Mo, T. Makishima, et al., 2002, "Dominant and recessive deafness caused by mutations of a novel gene, *TMC1*, required for cochlear hari-cell function," *Nat. Genet.* 30, 277-84.

106. T.R. Prezant, J.V. Agapian, M.C. Bohlman, X. Bu, S. Oztas, W.Q. Qiu, K.S. Arnos, G.A. Cortopassi, L. Jaber, J.I. Rotter, et al. 1993, "Mitochondrial ribosomal RNA mutation associated with both antibiotic induced and non-syndromic deafness," *Nat. Genet.*, 4, 289-94.

107. M.X. Guan, N. Fishel-Ghodsian and G. Attardi, 2001, "Nuclear background determines biochemical phenotype in the deafness-associated mitochondrial 12S RNA mutation," *Hum. Mol. Genet.*, 10, 573-80.

108. R.G. Weleber, R.E. Carr, W.H. Murphy, V.C. Sheffield and E.M. Stone, 1993, "Phenotypic variation retinitis pigmentosa, pattern dystrophy and fundus flavimaculatus in a single family with a deletion of codon 153 or 154 of the Peripherin/RDS Gene," *Arch. Opthal.*, 111, 1531-42.

109. S.G. Jacobson, A.V. Cideciyan, A. Iannaccone, R.G. Weleber, G.A. Fishman, A.M. Maguire, L.M. Affatigato, J. Bennett, E.A. Pierce, M. Danciger, et al., 2000, "Disease expression of PR1 mutations causing autosomal dominant retintis pigmentosa," *Invest. Ophthalmol. Vis. Sci.* 41., 1898-1908.

110. J.E. Craig, P.N. Baird, D.L. Healey, A.I. McNaught, P.J. McCartney, J.L. Rait, J.L. Dickinson, L. Roe, J.H. Fingert, E.M.

Stone, and D.A. Mackey, 2001, "Evidence for genetic heterogenetity within eight glaucoma families, with the GLC1A Gln 368STOP mutation being an important phenotypic modifier," *Opthalmol*, 108, 1607-20.

111. R. Riise, S. Andreasson, M.K. Borgastrom, A.F. Wright, N. Tommerup, T. Rosenberg and K. Tornqvist, 1997, "Intrafamilial variation of the phenotype in Bardet-Biedl syndrome," *Br. J. Ophthalmol.*, 81, 378-85.

112. R. Carmi, K. Elbedour, E.M. Stone and V.C. Sheffield, 1995, "Phenotypic differences among patients with Bardet-Biedl syndrome linked to three different chromosome loci," *Am. J. Med. Genet*, 59, 199-203.

113. A.M. Slavotinek, E.M. Stone, K. Mykytyn, J.R. Heckenlively, J.S. Green, E. Heon, M.A. Musarella, P.S. Parfrey, V.C. Sheffield and L.G. Biesecker, 2000, "Mutations in MKKS cause Bardet-Biedl syndrome," *Nat. Genet*, 26, 15-16.

114. N. Katsanis, S.J. Ansley, J.L. Badano, E.R. Eichers, R.A. Lewis, B.E. Hoskins, P.J. Scambler, W.S. Davidson, P.L. Beales and J.R. Lupski, 2001, "Triallelic inheritance in Bardet-Biedl syndrome, a Mendelian recessive disorder," *Science*, 293, 2256-59.

115. A.H. Burghes, H.E. Vaessin, and A. de La Chapelle, 2001, "Genetics, The land between Mendelian and multifactorial inheritance," Science, 293, 2213-14.

References

Bargmann, C.I., 1999, A complex sensory map for pheromones," *Neuron*, 22, 640-42.

Firestein, S., 2001, "How the olfactory system makes sense of scents," *Nature*, 413, 211-18.

Fischel-Ghodsian, N., 1999, "Motochondrial deafness mutations reviewed," *Hum. Mutat.*, 13, 261-70.

Kolakiowski, L.F. Jr., 1994, "GCRDb: A Gprotein-coupled receptor database, Recept," *Channels* 2(1): 1-7.

18

Modern Technology to Imitate Five Senses

Ajeya Jha
H.K.D. Sarma

LIVING beings are said to be alive, that is they differ from non-living beings, by virtue of the five senses they possess. Some may not have one or the other sense organs; as many burrowing creatures are bind; even the creatures that have evolved in dark caves have lost their sense of vision. Bats are blind and so on, but by and large they possess sense-organs, even the most insignificant unicellular ones too. Keenness of senses too differ from creature to creature. Human beings are believed to have exceptionally evolved senses of vision and taste. Most animals are colour-blind to a certain extent, but human beings can readily recognize even the slightest tinge of colour difference. (Although modern studies have shown that certain birds have richer vision than human beings in terms of perceiving colour.) Sense of smell of dogs is legendary. Human beings cannot distinguish other fellow human beings by their smells, but dogs do. Even their sense of hearing is far more advanced than that of human beings. Further there are sounds that we cannot even perceive. The sound created by bats (as they are above a frequency of 20,000) is inaudible to us, so is the sound emitted by elephants in distress (it is below a frequency of 20).

Why do creatures differ in terms of their sense-organs? Scientists suggest that it could be because of the different environment they have to survive in.

Man is different in also being far more intelligent than other animals and aspires to overcome all his limitations through intelligence. In his quest to excel he found a significant tool in the shape of electronics. One of the endeavours of researchers involved with electronics is to establish artificial intelligence. Now intelligence presumes senses, as without senses there will be no input to analyse or take decisions. Thus a major part of research on artificial intelligence is related to developing artificial sense-organs. How successful we have been so far in this field? Are there any limitations that cannot be overcome by technology? What will be the eventual shape of the artificial sense-organs being designed? And most importantly what will be its impact on the human philosophies, social, cultural and psychological aspects of life? These are a few questions that need to exploration. This paper attempts find answers to these questions.

Before answering these questions a little introduction of the advances that have taken place will be relevant to this discussion.

The application of multivariate data analysis combined with sensors and partially overlapping selectivities has become a very powerful tool in measurement technology. These systems are often referred to as artificial senses, because they function in a way similar to the human senses. Artificial sense technologies make use of various types of sensors. A sensor is an entity that tells something about its environment. An electronic sensor is a sensor that gives information about its environment by creating an electrical signal. This signal should change as the entity it is measuring changes.

Electronic Feelers

Electronic feelers are sensors that are designed to mimic the sense of touch. We are able to discern hot-cold, hard-soft, smooth-rough, dry-damp, heavy-light because of the inherent sense of touch we possess. Electronic sensors that are being designed to substitute human sense of touch measure many environmental factors such as heat, humidity, weight, hardness, roughness, etc. A heat sensor, for example, measures the temperature of any object and converts this into an electronic signal the intensity of which can be measured. Further depending upon the values of measurement a decision signal (switch on/switch off) is then sent down wires, back to the heater itself.

Each of the parameters mentioned earlier require different types of sensors. Each sensor operates on a more or less unique technology. It can be simple or complicated, but eventually they translate their signals to something that can be sent down a wire, or sent over a radio wave.

Electronic Nose

The "electronic nose" is a more or less recent tool. The technology it involves is built around two components:

- An assortment of chemical sensors (usually gas sensors), and
- A pattern-recognition algorithm.

A smell that is to be recognized or distinguished is measured against a smell-bank. The sensor assortment "smells" the vapours from a sample and provides a set of measurements, the pattern-recognizer compares the pattern of the measurements to the smell of known materials stored in the smell-bank.

Electronic nose is finding use in industries for safety, quality, or process monitoring. There are instances that an electronic nose could reduce operation time for a procedure from a few days to a fraction of a second. Scientists have developed a device which will save lives by smelling tuberculosis-causing bacteria. Determining the presence of these bacteria, otherwise, requires a few days.

Electronic Tongue

Electronic nose discussed earlier is related to olfaction. Based on similar electronic principles it is possible for electronic equipment to identify, distinguish or measure "taste." The e-tongue has been designed by the electronic engineers to be the structural equivalent of the human tongue. Human tongue comprises four different types of receptors that respond to distinct tastes. Thousands of tastes stored in a biological brain are matched against the pattern created by human tongue to recall the taste of a particular food.

To e-tongue comprises 10 to 100 polymer microbeads positioned on a silicon chip that is one centimetre square. Beads are arranged in tiny pits to represent taste buds. Each pit is dyed to create a red, green and blue (RGB) colour bar. The colours change when the scientists introduce chemicals to the e-tongue. A camera on a chip connected to a computer then examines the colours and performs a simple RGB analysis that in turn determines what tastes are present. Yellow, for example, would be a response to high acidity, or a sour taste.

Electronic tongues are known to distinguish tastes that are not discernible by human taste faculty.

The food and beverage industries are looking forward to using the tongue to develop a digital library of tastes proven to be popular with consumers, or to monitor the flavours of existing products. It is believed that the electronic tongue eventually may replace human tasters. It could be of use for unconventional situations too. The e-tongue is known to "taste" cholesterol levels in blood, cocaine in urine, or toxins in water.

Various measurement principles that are used in electronic tongues include electro-chemical techniques such as potentiometry, voltammetry and conductometry. Optical techniques based on light absorption at specific wave lengths or mass-sensitive devices based on piezoelectric crystals also find application for building electronic tongues.

Electronic Eye

Electronic eye represents many types of technologies developed to mimic human eye. It could be as simple as to acquire (scan, capture by digital cameras) digital images to compare and analyse them for characteristics that a human eye alone couldn't perceive. This ability to perceive minute variations is quite useful when trying to identify a person by comparing his/her picture against million others. It has been shown to be effective even if a person has aged considerably since the photograph was taken.

However, the technology involves even more powerful aspirations — to capture visual signals, analyse them and then take decisions based on inference; all this to take place in a fraction of a second. An example would be a driverless car. Such a technology involves use of a camera that takes pictures at the rate of ten frames per second. These photographs are continually processed with the help of sophisticated algorithms. How much do we think we know about real time?

Electronic Ear

Speech processing and speech recognition are two aspects of electronic ear. The human hearing system involves two processes:

- System to receive the vibrations of a sound,
- Analysis of vibrations in the brain to recognize it and initiate appropriate instructions to the muscles.

A live example would be giving instructions to a computer via a voice processor. Specific software drives such a system. A microphone converts speech into a signal (because of pressure variations) which is represented with the help of a pulse code modulator technique. In other words the voice is digitalized (changed into 0 and 1 category).

Another application is bionic ear — an artificial hearing device, designed to produce useful hearing. The present-day multi-channel bionic ear consists of 2 main components: (1) the cochlear implant package and electrode array (or receiver-stimulator); and (2) the speech processor and headset.

Speech and other sounds are picked up by the microphone and sent to the speech processor. The processor codes the sounds into an electrical signal which is sent via a cable to the transmitting coil (which is held in place by a magnet). The coil then passes the signal through the skin via radio waves to the implant which transforms the signal into electrical pulses. The radio waves also provide power to the implant, as there is no battery in the internal part. The pulses pass from the electrode array and stimulate the hearing nerve fibres within the cochlear.

The speech processor does not just make sounds louder like a hearing aid. Instead, it selects out some of the important information in the speech signal and then produces a pattern of electrical pulses in the patient's ear. This pattern is selected to be as close as possible to the original speech sound. It is not possible to make sounds completely natural, because there are only 22 electrodes that are replacing the function of tens of thousands of hair cells in a normally hearing ear.

Discussion

How do these technologies compare with the natural human sense organs? Are they as good or even better?

To begin with, these are quite expensive technologies as yet. Further their real time application is a challenge. High-efficiency for complicated cases is impossible as yet. Developing algorithms for such technologies is arduous and requires excellect imagination.

An example would be a car that was developed by Massachusetts Institute of Technology (MIT). It had a camera fitted in front of it which took 10-12 pictures per second, which was not enough as car could move slowly. The "mind" in car was programmed to steer the car depending upon the difference in colour of road and the pavement. For some time it moved smoothly but then it came across a small patch of snow. Since here the colour of road and pavement is the same (snow white) the car lost its sense of balance and moved towards a pond and went inside it.

This example goes on to show the extreme versatility of mind. Computer-driven machines can solve known problems but human mind not only uses the information stored in the brain but also finds ways to solve the unknown and the unstructured problems. Future research may gift us with artificial senses much more powerful than human mind but while confronting unstructured and ambiguous situations human solutions will be better.

In search for artificial intelligence, the electronics researchers have hit a road block. The only way to have intelligence of higher order is to understand how human mind works. But the biologists do not yet know how our brain functions. It is a mystery which refuses to be unravelled.

Further there is human instinct — the culmination of wealth of experience we have inherited from our ancestors in the last thousands of years that are stored in our subconscious and unconscious mind. Can artificial intelligence find their equivalent?

Then we are blessed with a conscience — an intense, deep-seated and a vibrant sense of right and wrong. Can artificial sense refuse to be operated by an evil person? After all ethics are more essential for our survival and growth than intelligence. As Martin Luther King commented:

> Our scientific powers have outrun our spiritual powers,
> We have guided missiles and unguided men.

And last, but not the least, are our emotions — the positive ones. Human beings are motivated by love the most. Can artificial intelligence ever be a Buddha, a Gandhi or a Mother Teresa? Saint Kabir had said a few centuries back:

> A man may read books after books, yet remain a fool,
> But the one who learns to love — attains enlightenment.

This is not to run down the excellent work that scientists are performing in the area of artificial intelligence. This is only to spell out that human faculties will be essential for future peace and prosperity for all. The artificial senses at best can be complementary to our natural abilities but will never be a just substitute for them.

19

Socio-cultural Construction of Senses and the Post-modern Society

Umesh K. Singh

THE concept of senses has evolved through the history of mankind in different connotations and implications. Though senses are purely biophysical phenomena, yet their governing properties lie in the cognitive map which the human civilization has evolved from primitive to modern world. The primordial man had the same senses which the post-modern man has today. Yet the faculty of senses has evolved newer dimensions as the human civilization progressed. The meanings attached to the perceptual cognition have always varied. The culture to which a human group belongs has defined the implications of what we perceive, listen, touch, etc. (Classen, et al., 1994). The term *sense* is not an absolute phenomenon. It is a relative concept depending upon an individual's level of sense perception, his consciousness, his cognition, and his intentions and volitions. In the primitive society, meanings were attached to sense objects within the common parameters prevalent in its particular culture. Similarity and uniformity were the dominant features of such sense perceptions. However, the primitive notion changed when the society became more differentiated, atomized and individualistic (Classen, 1993). Within the same culture in such societies the result of the perceptual cognition also became differentiated and individualistic. The tremendous growth in human knowledge, new discoveries and inventions in the field of science and technology has enlarged cognition and vision of mankind. This cognition and vision of post-industrial society is a watershed in providing an enlarged canvas to our cognition and sense perception. Nineteenth and twentieth centuries have been characterized by such phenomena where sense perception was not limited to bio-physical arena, not even to the cultural context of the individuals and communities, but was determined and defined by the post-industrial social order. This has led to differentiation between traditional man and modern man. Whereas the sense perception of the traditional man was simply organic and replicatory, the sense perception of post-industrial man has become increasingly differentiated and technocratic. Moreover, the perceptual cognition of the traditional man was more inner-directed which changed over to other-directed cognitive person in contemporary times. In the post-industrial era a new phenomenon entered into the cognitive world — the concept of class consciousness which proclaimed the dominance of existence over the being. The materialist conditions of life divided society into different economic strata. This became the governing property of cognition and sense perception in the Marxian era (Synnott, 1991). It also proclaimed that the cognitive world of different strata can be altered through well-directed and organized propaganda devices. Even the objective conditions of life may be transformed and this may lead to an entirely new cognitive map. For a considerable long time, the Marxian conception of class-consciousness lasted and all the non-materialist explanations of the cognitive world were outrightly rejected. Norms, values, ideas and institutions were categorized on the basis of these non-materialist and materialist explanations. The traditional notion of ideational culture gave place to materialist interpretation of external world.

The World of Senses

Though all the five major senses reveal the outside reality, yet the same senses may also lead to esoteric knowledge which is not external. However, the perceived reality is always multi-layered and multi-dimensional.

The five major senses have definite functions to perform. The senses are functionally related to one's cognition and knowledge. But each of these senses has its own place which is sometimes hierarchically graded and can be termed as lower and higher senses (Synnott, 1993). Moreover the sense which comes through touch may be sensuous and pleasure-giving (Fisher, 1997) which reflects the lower status of touch sensations. At the same time the touch which produces a musical tone or supernatural feelings may be termed as higher level of touch sensation. The eye beholds the inner beauty and it can produce only pleasant or unpleasant reaction in men. Olfactory senses too have the two-dimensional cognition of reality (Drobnick, 1998; Howes, 1991). Sound possesses more sophisticated production of the reality and it can also lead to baser realities. Taste has the similar property. It has the material dimension where anything edible either becomes acceptable, palatable or repulsive. The human life has evolved around these functional roles of senses. However, the same senses when they become extra-sensory perception, spiritual awakening, telepathy, premonition, astral projection are not easily comprehensible phenomena. The ordinary mortals do not possess or are not able to discern such developed faculties. Whereas the same mortal being when he attains higher level of awakening, he leads to sublime, divine or highly spiritual stage of cognition. The higher level of cognition has occurred among saints, mendicants, spiritual leaders and prophets of any religion of the world. Not only their awakening through rigorous spiritual training has resulted in the enhancement of the power of senses but through these they have attained a higher level of consciousness where even the revealed knowledge becomes a reality.

The multi-layered role of sense faculty could be seen in human beings where one faculty may be dormant and the other faculties may be performing higher tasks of cognition which are otherwise not being performed by sense faculties in other human beings. Braille has enabled a blind person to understand the world around him. The blind has not only become a lettered human being but a person who can even perceive the colour. Medical advances have enabled the spastic, the deaf and the dumb to understand the outside reality. The role of improved psychological techniques and the related technological advances have enabled the mentally disabled person to be more closely in touch with the outside world.

Thus ranging from a super individual's faculties of human senses to the artificially created and technologically added devices, the human senses have produced a wide spectrum of knowledge and cognition of reality. The intervention of technology in contemporary times has enlarged the physical and mental ability of the individual which though appear to be artificial and contrived, yet it helps the physically and mentally impaired to face the outer reality through providing a new contextual apparatus of knowledge.

Five Senses in Different Cultures

Aesthetics related to human behaviour has always been a crucial area of debate (Barrett, 1988; Eagleton, 1990). Senses shape the human behaviour and the human behaviour may be good or bad. Thus, the senses get involved in the labelling of human behaviour in hierarchically graded categories of altruistic or debased. Some of the human sense faculties have been associated with the baser elements of human nature while others are associated with its refinement and cultivation. The senses like touch, smell and taste have been typed as too primitive (Classen, 1998). Both the aboriginals of the primordial societies and the so-called civilized human beings of the contemporary cultures have enjoyed the outside world through the senses in such baser manners which are considered to be barbaric, sensuous and sexually perverted aspects of human behaviour. The aboriginals who were illiterate and considered as uncultivated and uncultured, utilized these inferior senses for non-human and crude forms of behaviour. These inferior senses even in the modern times could be used and have been used for the same baser elements of behaviour even though the human being of the contemporary society is considered "much advanced," "much civilized," and "much literate" as compared to the aboriginals. Why this similarity in the use of primitive senses between the aboriginals and the modern men? Human civilization has registered considerable advancement in the realm of aesthetics but the perversion of human primitive senses has remained the same. Does it mean that the inferior senses should be outrightly rejected? Does it imply that in order to achieve aesthetic perfection and higher values, the inferior senses should be sidetracked? The answer lies in the field of human experience in different cultures and different modes of behaviour. The society is multi-layered and the cultures differ from one place and time to the other. The so-called inferior senses can be "good" in one particular culture and social stratum. The working class aesthetics of the contemporary society is entirely different than the highbrow culture of the bourgeois society. Yet the working class aesthetics related to the inferior senses is as good as that of bourgeois culture. The change in the context can make a vital difference in the resultant effects of the inferior senses.

Though senses which are construed as higher senses possess a very high status in the aesthetics and hierarchies of values, they have their own problem. Higher senses do have the properties of refinement and cultivation yet they are not outright perfect and absolute in nature. They have relativity of their own. Perceiving the external object or deciphering its inner meaning or hidden value is not the same in all human beings howsoever elevated they may be. The attainment of spiritual consciousness and the exploration into the esoteric meaning of the things and actions differ from person to person. Is it only a difference related to psychic capability of the individual or is it the function of socio-cultural or religious capabilities of the individual or the group to which he belongs, is difficult to discern. The attainment of higher sense ability would also be not called a *sādhanā* or any such arduous training of human mind. There have been instances where revelations, visions and hidden meanings have surfaced to people even without any rigorous mental training. Why such differences occur still remains a mystery of human senses. Sometimes, it is the individual who becomes the centripetal force in the journey towards the unknown. At other times it is the function of culture which makes the difference in the attainment of higher level senses. The higher senses in their rudiments remain a socio-psychological mystical experience.

One of the most amazing roles being performed by senses in different cutural contexts related to their healing power. Touch, gaze and hearing are three major sense faculties which are closely related to healing power. In all the traditional religions, sound is one such area which creates vibrations and energies which go on to contribute rejuvenation, cure and spiritual elevation. The sound of *oṁ* in Hinduism, *oṁ maṇi padme huṁ* in Buddhism, *allāh hu akbar* in Islam and the chanting of *mantra*s, hymns and other prayers in Hinduism, Buddhism and Jainism perform the same miraculous role among the believers of a particular tradition. The sound may be created by a person or by some cultural artefacts producing a different type of healing effect which though anchored in the faith, results in certain concrete material benefits for the believers.

Similarly, touch has got different cultural connotations in the context of healing process. Apart from the role of touch as used in acupressure, acupuncture and other traditional healing arts, the simple touch of a seer, shaman, *maulavī* or priest has got a different connotation in the art of healing. Many ailments especially the psychic diseases are supposed to be cured by touch. Touch may register high or low response depending upon the level of spiritual attainment and healing power of the individual practitioner.

Gaze too has got the same importance in the art of healing. It is rather a difficult art to be attained by the individual practitioner. In South-East Asian healing system, especially in China and in India, gaze has been recognized as the very important process through which the individual practitioner can penetrate into the psyche of the person who is being observed and some super energy gets transferred from the practitioner to the observed one. Apart from gazing into the eyes of the person, gaze is also a method of knowing the unknown by perceiving things in crystal, utensil, water and some other ingredients put in the healing pot. All the foregoing healing role of the senses may or may not be proved clinically. Yet in the kingdom of faith, these senses have got immense power. The believers do feel the benefit out of these healing touch, gaze and sound.

Optical Illusions of the Modern and the Post-modern Times

Modern Western culture is a culture of the eye. The images in forms of visual models and representations are there to seduce and shape us by their invariant bombardment by the popular media of today. To a large extent, the global cultural flows of our time are generated and directed by global media empires that rely on powerful communication technologies to spread their message. Saturating global cultural reality with formulaic TV shows and mindless advertisements, these corporations increasingly shape people's identities and the structure of desires around the world (Steger, 2003). Though many of the contemporary manifestations of visual media like advertisements, etc. seem to have a distinctive but intangible quality of rationality and objectivity, however they are designed to manipulate the emotions more than to exercise the reason. The visual nature of much of the present representation helps maintain this aura of objectivity by appearing to provide the viewer with direct access to reality, rather than only mediating reality (Classen, 1998).

Growing abstraction of the evolution of image production in post-modern times brings out the alienating effects of image making in a techno-capitalist society. What had been a society has imploded into a hyperconformist body obsessed so much with spectacle that it would rather watch TV than take political action (Baudrillard, 1983). We are today confronted not so much with the alienation of our senses (this being a typically modern phenomenon) as with the sensualization of alienation. In other words, post-modernity has economized sensuality as such; it has turned the image into a commodity and by this has hollowed out our perception of reality (Beller, 2003).

The visualist regime of the present era, in fact, prides itself on its transparency (Vattimo, 1992). Our inquisitive and acquisitive eyes can see everything and can know everything — nothing is withheld. The microscopic view and panoramic view intersect to display our world to us inside and out. The gaze is elevated into great importance, as a power associated with the eye and the sense of sight. When we *gaze* at things, our aim is to control them. In case of surveillance by means of the "panopticon": for the observer, sight confers power; for the observed, visibility is powerlessness (Ashcroft et al., 2004).

However, the very visualism of today has, so to speak, thrown a cloak of invisibility over the sensory imagery of previous eras. So thick is this cloak that one can scarcely see through it, or even recognize that there might be something worth exploring underneath. We seem to have forgotten that vision is a social phenomenon and it is always socially groomed. People have not seen identically throughout history. Vision changes as political and economic circumstances do (Cavallaro, 2001). Moreover, although sight, as a means to knowledge and control of ourselves and others, is regarded the most important of the five senses, however, the other senses are equally important. To explore how taste, touch, smell and sound are deeply implicated in ethical and cultural systems and to savour the multi-sensory splendour of the cosmos, we have to lift the cloak of visualism of today. Classen (1998) puts it rather nicely:

> The aesthetic cornucopia of earlier cosmologies was not simply a hedonistic revelling in sensation. The myriad sensory characteristics of such cosmologies, their colours and odours, tastes and temperatures, were coded with cultural values and linked in chains and hierarchies of meaning. The visual was an important element in this construction of sensory meaning, but it was not all-encompassing. If often first in line as the "noblest" of the senses, sight none the less took its place alongside the other senses, without subsuming them. The multiplicity of sensory channels of communication meant that one could taste or breathe in the order of the cosmos and society, as well as visualize it.

Senses in the Futuristic Society

However, there is another crucial dimension too. So far we were speaking about the senses of ordinary human beings, about our own senses of sight, hearing, smell, taste, etc. However, it is likely that human beings, as we know them, will undergo profound alteration. The changes taking place in our society are so radical that they are likely to affect the essence of being human (Heylighen, 1997).

In cyberspace people immersed in a virtual environment can actually experience the realistic feeling of inhabiting that world. The user of Virtual Reality receives images and impressions from various mechanical devices attached to the user's body, to provide the impressions of sight, sound and touch.

We are in the era of cybernetics where possibility to design machines which replicate the human organism is being explored. This cybernetic organism mirrors the human body not in the simplicity of ways of conventional robots but on the basis of an understanding of the structural similarity between machines and living organisms.

There seem to be possibilities of people evolving into "post-humans," whose basic capacities so radically exceed those of present humans as to be no longer unambiguously human by our current standards. Post-humans could be artificial intelligence, or they could be uploaded consciousness, or they could be the result of making many smaller but cumulatively profound augmentations to a biological human. The latter alternative would probably require either the redesign of the human organism using advanced nanotechnology or its radical enhancement using some combination of technologies such as genetic engineering, psychopharmacology, anti-ageing therapies, neural interfaces, advanced information management tools, memory enhancing drugs, wearable computer and cognitive techniques. Others see the emergence of "cyborgs," human-machine hybrids, which are supposed to be more flexible than the human organism. The cyborg embodies the idea that there are no clear divisions between the non-human and the human, the technological and the biological, the artificial and the natural (Carvallaro, 2001).

Moreover in the present era of medical and technological advancement, cosmetic surgery, biotechnology, genetic engineering and the replacement of organic functions by biochip implants show that there is simply no such thing as a *pure body*, and consequently the conventional wisdom about the human senses may get eroded. This further raises a serious consideration for the future of senses. This involves rediscovering and reimagining our senses in the context of ever-changing technology and its relationship with the individual human being placed in the growing complexity of modern times.

References

Ashcroft, B., G. Griffiths and H. Tiffin, 2004, *Key Concepts in Post-Colonial Studies*, London: Routledge.

Barrett, M., 1988, "The Place of the Aesthetic in Marxist Criticism," in C. Nelson and L. Grossberg (eds.), *Marxism and the Interpretation of Culture*, pp. 697-715, Urbana and Chicago: University of Illinois Press.

Baudrillard, J., 1983, *In the Shadow of the Silent Majorities . . . or the End of the Social and Other Essays*, New York: Semiotext.

Beller, J.L., 2003, "Numismatics of the Sensual, Calculus of the Image: The Pyrotechnics of Control," *Image & Narrative — Online Magazine of the Visual Narrative*, vol. 6.

Cavallaro, D., 2001, *The Body For Beginners*, Chennai: Orient Longman.

Classen, C., 1993, *Worlds of Sense: Exploring the Senses in History and Across Cultures*, London: Routledge.

Classen, C., 1998, *The Color of Angels: Cosmology, Gender and the Aesthetic Imagination*, London and New York: Routledge.

Classen, C., D. Howes and A. Synnott, 1994, *Aroma: The Cultural History of Smell*, London: Routledge.

Drobnick, J., 1998, Reveries, Assaults and evaporating presences: Olfactory dimesions in contemporary art, *Parachute* #89, Winter 1998, pp. 10-19.

Eagleton, T., 1990, *The Ideology of the Aesthetic*, Oxford: Basil and Blackwell Ltd. Fisher, J., 1997, Relational Sense: Towards a Haptic Aesthetics, *Parachute* # 87, pp. 4-11.

Heylighen, F., 1997: Towards a Global Brain, Integrating Individuals into the World-Wide Electronic Network, Published in German as: "Auf dem Weg zum 'Global Brain'. Der Mensch im weltweiten electronischen Netz," in U. Brandes and C. Neumann (eds.), *Der Sinn der Sinne*, pp. 302-18. Göttingen: Steidl Verlag.

Howes, D., 1991," Olfaction and Transition," in D. Howes (ed.), *The Varieties of Sensory Experience: A Sourcebook in the Anthropology of the Senses*, pp. 128-47, Toronto: University of Toronto Press.

Steger, M.B., 2003, *Globalization — A Very Short Introduction*, New York: Oxford University Press.

Synnott, A., 1991, "Puzzling Over the Senses: From Plato to Marx," in D. Howes (ed.), *The Varieties of Sensory Experience: A Sourcebook in the Anthropology of the Senses*, pp. 61-76., Toronto: University of Toronto Press.

Synnott, A., 1993, *The Body Social: Symbolism, Self and Society*, London: Routledge.

Vattimo, G., 1992, *The Transparent Society*, Cambridge: Polity Press.

20

The Five Senses Theory

Henrik Janne

Who sets the Five Senses in order?

NATURE, because in it there are codes already preprogrammed about how everything should look, smell, feel, sound and taste. That is, in Nature there are laws for how exactly it all (on supposition that this everything is organic, but on the other hand, it does not even have to be organic, it could also be a rock), should "be born" and how it should be fitted together into a whole. These laws or seeds to everything have already been made accounted for, so to speak, by Nature. These are the so-called laws of Nature, which can even be seen on a molecular level via modern technology, as extremely complex patterns or even smaller, tiny particles in collaboration. Moreover, one can observe these laws of Nature in DNA. Or even better, one can go out in the Nature, wilderness, and perceive Nature (the laws) via one's own Five senses. So, the laws of Nature sets the Five senses in order due to the fact that humans, who contain these Five senses, are a part of this Nature.

But this raises the question: Who/What sets the Nature in order? This is, to my point of view, an even more problematic question to answer (not meaning that the first one was easy!). Hence, I only will make a foolish walk around the well of knowledge, and try to look down into it.

Nature is supreme, the ultimate, and the end of the line. Nature is the Supreme Being or the Supreme Form of consciousness. That is, everything is consciousness. Because Nature is everything. Now, could one compare Nature with God? I certainly think so. Because to me, Nature is equal to the Supreme form of consciousness, or if you will, God. So, the answer to the above question would be, from my point of view, that Nature sets Nature in order. Because Nature is the Supreme form of consciousness, which sustains itself. Nature has its own form of janitors so to speak, that puts grease in its own machinery. Or less materialistically put, waves ponder the seashore to make it erosive, earth melts into the ocean. New earth comes up from down below and will eventually once again fall down into it.

Where is the seed of the archaic?

In Nature, and in its Supreme form of consciousness, inside the laws of Nature. These laws contain the seeds of the archaic.

How do we look at the individual self?

We humans look at our individual selves through self-imagination and with our ability to connect this self-imagination to our direct reality, i.e. the surrounding environment which we simultaneously act within. Some people use a "better technique" for self-viewing and some people are not so sensitive for this matter. That is, the latter mentioned are easier to fool, if one takes media and/or the commercial/advertisement aspect to mind. Further on, the former "kind" of people have a better tuned and better self-realism, self-distance, which I believe is crucial for a healthy self-image. That is, to look at the individual self in a more sensible and subtle way. And further on, I believe we use our ability to fantasize and dream (both day and night) about ourselves in accordance to our ongoing environment, but this is a very floating way of putting it, perhaps. Because this is a subconsciously ongoing apparatus, which not everyone is aware of that they are using. This does not mean that it does not exist and, primarily, that it does not serve a function in everyday life. It only means this, some people are aware and some people are not aware about this life-sustaining ability or natural self-preservation instinct.

Now this also implies that we use a form of internal perception to observe the individual self. With internal perception I mean a form of inverted "outer" perception. Where there is a plus-pole (external perception due to the five senses) there must be a minus-pole (internal perception due to "the internal five senses"). The external perception and inverted perception is connected and interrelated to: awareness about oneself's feelings, self-respect, self-reliability, self-consciousness, self-image, consciousness about oneself in relation to: Psychosocial-geographical-historical-cultural-economical and not the least religious environments. Here there is a psychodynamic aspect of perception, and how we look at the individual self.

And furthermore, generally, often we look at the individual self according to how we think we ought to look at our individual self, subconciously. That is, in accordance to phychosocial conventions about how people, in general, "should" see themselves, the individual self. Probably this is due to the "mass-media-flow" and the way views, opinions and even how one should feel about something are implemented into human mind. This, I believe, is due to "the fact" that people are very anxious about fitting into the general aspect of living (which media moguls are too aware of!). How they should dress, act, speak and even how they should think fits this subconscious purpose. Because individuals, all individual selves, humans, are beings of a flock or better put it, humans are "flock-animals." It is a great need of humans, conformity, and the feeling of recognition. This aspect also fits into the psychodynamics of human mind. And finally, this is even more another way of looking at the individual self.

Chinese Rock Art:
Courtesy: Chen Zhao Fu and B.N. Saraswati, 1994

fig. 1
Praying Figures: Yunan, China

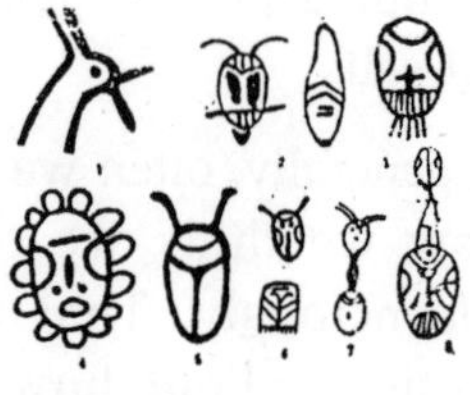

fig. 2
Masks Reflected Spiritualhead World : Northern China

*fig.*3
Rock Engraving : Helanshan, Ninxia

The Contributors

Manojit Debnath, presented a simplified form of knowledge regarding plant's response to external stimulus.

Somasish Ghosh Dastidar, presented a simplified form of knowledge regarding plant's response to external stimulus.

Hikotaro Furuta, introduces Japan as one of the nations having highest sensitivity in the world.

A.S. Inam Shastri, is a Professor of Social Work at the Mahatma Gandhi Kashi Vidyapeeth, Varanasi.

Henrik Janne raises the question: who sets the Five Senses in order? and gives Nature as the answer.

Ajeya Jha, is a Scientist associated with the Manipal Institute of Technology, Majhital, Rangpo 737 132, Sikkim.

Niradbaran Mandal, is convinced that from ancient time the sages have grasped the Five Senses, giving logical foundation to consciousness and seeing without matter.

Kalpika Mukherjee, finds the functional sense-organs as aesthetic perception.

Arttatrana Nayak, deals with the conceptual understanding of the Chinese theory of "*Yin* and *Yang*."

S.N. Ojha, deals with bioinformatics of perception.

Sanghamitra Pal, reflects on the sense organs in the snake-catching technology of the Sapure Mal.

S.K. Pathak, deals with the key features of human senses described in the Budhhist Abhidharma text.

Onkar Prasad, is an anthropologist who deals with the tribal world.

Saroj Kr. Pyne, studies animal behaviour during natural disaster.

Sitansu Ray, has dealt with Rabindranath Tagore's congregational addresses on the Five Senses.

K.N. Sahay, is an anthropologist who deals with divine and demonic properties. He has been a Professor of Anthropology at the Ranchi University, Ranchi.

Gautam Samanta, studies animal behaviour during natural disaster.

Baidyanath Saraswati, is an anthropologist and founder of the N.K. Bose Memorial foundation at Varanasi.

H.K.D. Sarma, is a Scientist associated with the Manipal Institute of Technology, Majhitar, Rangpo 737 132, Sikkim.

Umesh K. Singh, is a Sociologist associated with Kanpur University.

Bashistha Narayan Sinha, is one of the greatest Jainologists in India and former Asst. Professor, Department of Philosophy, Mahatma Gandhi Kashi Vidhyapitha, Varanasi.

D.M. Solomon, is known for Christian understanding of Five Senses and the Bible.

B.D. Tripathi, is an eminent Sociologist and a former Professor of Mahatma Gandhi Kashi Vidyapeeth, Varanasi.

Uma Marina Vesci, came to India in 1963 to begin a new life that few scholars have the courage to undertake, to ponder the words of ancient Sanstrit.

Index

Other Books of Interest

Voice of Death — Traditional Thought and Modern Science; edited by **Baidyanath Saraswati.**

Published in association with N.K. Bose Memorial Foundation, Varanasi.

2005, vi, 226 p.; Index; 23 cm.

ISBN 81-246-0274-3 (Hb)

This book, presents an in-depth study of the concept of death from the distinct viewpoints of all religions and cultures and at the same time taking into account their common concept of continuity of life after death, in contrary to the biological science that adheres to the mechanism of "cell-death."

Voice of Life — Traditional Though and Modern Science; edited by **Baidyanath Saraswati**.

Published in association with N.K. Bose Memorial Foundation, Varanasi.

2006, vi, 151 p.; Index; 23 cm.

ISBN 81-246-0366-9 (Hb)

The book presents views on life from the traditional as well as modern perspectives to come up with many interpretations surveys evolution of life and extinction theories, focusing on development of life over 600 million years from simple to complex. The contributors delve into the Upanisadic and Vedic concepts of life, and the Hindu astrological and ayurvedic perception and Christian perspective of life as well.

मृत्यु की दस्तक – प्राचीन षास्त्र एवं आधुनिक ज्ञान; संपादक : बैद्यनाथ सरस्वती, रामलखन मौर्य।

निर्मल कुमार बोस स्मारक प्रतिश्ठान, वाराणसी, की सहभागिता से प्रकाशित।

2005, vii, 208 p.; Index; 23 cm.

ISBN 81-246-0314-6 (Hb)

इस व्यारव्यान में विभिन्न वर्गों के प्रबुद्ध जनों ने मृत्यु – जीवात्मा के लिए सबसे बडा सत्य – की अवधारणा और उसके धार्मिक एवं दार्शनिक अभिप्राय का अवलोकन किया है। यहाँ मुख्यतः हिन्दू धर्म में मष्त्योपरान्तैभ्मागत श्राद्ध कर्मों की विधि इत्यादि पर भी प्रकाश डाला गया है, साथ ही 'क्लोनिंग' से जूझते मृत्यु के सामाजिक और वास्तविक अभिप्राय तथा अन्य समकालीन तथ्यों को उजागर करने का भी भरपूर प्रयास किया गया है।